THE REVOLUTIONARY WRITINGS OF

Alexander Hamilton

ALEXANDER HAMILTON

THE REVOLUTIONARY WRITINGS OF
Alexander Hamilton

Edited and with an Introduction by Richard B. Vernier

With a Foreword by Joyce O. Appleby

Liberty Fund

INDIANAPOLIS

This book is published by Liberty Fund, Inc., a foundation
established to encourage study of the ideal of a society of free and responsible
individuals.

𒑒𒀸 𒂼𒄄

The cuneiform inscription that serves as our logo and as
the design motif for our endpapers is the earliest-known written
appearance of the word "freedom" (*amagi*), or "liberty." It is taken from a
clay document written about 2300 B.C. in the Sumerian
city-state of Lagash.

C   10   9   8   7   6   5   4   3   2   1
P   10   9   8   7   6   5   4   3   2

Library of Congress Cataloging-in-Publication Data
Hamilton, Alexander, 1757–1804.
The revolutionary writings of Alexander Hamilton / edited and with an
introduction by Richard B. Vernier; with a foreword by Joyce O. Appleby.
p. cm.
Includes index.
ISBN 978-0-86597-705-1 (alk. paper)—ISBN 978-0-86597-706-8 (pbk. : alk. paper)
1. United States—Politics and government—1775–1783.   2. United States—
Politics and government—1783–1809.   3. United States—History—Revolution,
1775–1783.   4. Hamilton, Alexander, 1757–1804—Political and social views.
5. Political science—United States—History—18th century.   I. Vernier, Richard B.
II. Title.
E302.H22 2008
973.4092—dc22   2006052800

Liberty Fund, Inc.
8335 Allison Pointe Trail, Suite 300
Indianapolis, Indiana 46250-1684

CONTENTS

FOREWORD

Joyce O. Appleby

AMERICANS HAVE an unusual relationship to the founding era of their nation. They not only revere their many Founding Fathers but study their lives and writings with great avidity. Curators, scholars, and popular writers respond to this taste with exhibits, books, videos, and conferences. Bicentennial commemorations of the American Revolution began in 1975 and continued annually with reenactments, tours, and TV shows. Alexander Hamilton's death at the hand of Aaron Burr prompted a major exhibit in New York City in 2005; the tricentennial of Benjamin Franklin's birth was marked by a year-long celebration in Philadelphia in 2006.

Skeptics can verify this fascination by "googling" George Washington, Thomas Jefferson, Benjamin Franklin, John Adams, James Madison, Alexander Hamilton, and John Marshall, whose names pull up sites in the thousands. Online bookstores follow suit with hundreds of titles, many of which were written in the past decade.

Although most of the issues and values that divided America's leaders in the nation-building years of the late eighteenth century are remote from those that stir us today, the passions aroused by these old contests persist in the present. Readers often reveal a keen sense of partiality, if not partisanship, toward the revolutionary leaders. When Adams is riding high in popularity, esteem for Jefferson decreases. The same applies to Jefferson and Hamilton. As we move into a season of bicentennials of Marshall's great decisions, these too will probably provoke criticism of his rivals, Jefferson and Madison.

While clearly a Founding Father of great significance, Hamilton holds a somewhat eccentric relationship to these other central figures. He died young in a scandalous duel; he was never president; and his personal relations lacked the rectitude so noticeable in George Washington. He might have fit in better in the British Parliament, where he could conceivably have found a place, given his birth in the Caribbean colony of Nevis. Yet few American leaders have ever been better loved than Hamilton was by the young Federalists who looked to him to carry them back to their rightful place at the head of the nation until death cut short his brilliant political career.

What Hamilton had was genius, conspicuous even as a teenager. Extraordinary talent always attracts notice. Hamilton collected powerful patrons the way other young men acquire bad debts. His abundant gifts, well wrapped in personal discipline, earned him a passage from the island of St. Croix, where he worked as a shipping clerk, to New York City to study at Columbia, then called King's College. There Hamilton's quickness, wit, charm, and diligence won him a new group of enthusiastic backers who felt their faith in him well vindicated by his writings in support of the Patriot cause.

In a few years Hamilton passed from an academic prodigy to the most treasured of George Washington's aides-de-camp. Making himself nearly indispensable to Washington through his management of headquarters and report-writing, he also put together an intelligence network of spies in New York City, which the British occupied throughout the war. Despite Washington's reliance upon Hamilton as a secretary of the first order, Hamilton yearned for military action. Elevated to the rank of lieutenant-colonel, he managed to lead both an artillery and an infantry unit in important battles and finished his army career with a daring attack on one of the British positions at Yorktown.

Given to neither the studiousness of Madison nor the wide-ranging intellectual curiosity of Jefferson, Hamilton gravitated to the technical issues of governance. His moment came when Washington organized the first presidential administration under the new Constitution and chose him as secretary of the treasury. No man in the United States was as prepared as Hamilton to use the new federal powers to craft a series of mutually enhancing statutes dealing with taxes, trade, and the revolutionary debt. He possessed a strong political philosophy, congenial to the Federalists who gravitated around Washington but at odds with the increasingly popular democratic sentiments that triumphed with Jefferson's election in 1801 and the subsequent sweep of successive Congressional elections.

As the writings of this volume so well reveal, Hamilton was a natural rhetorician in the best sense of that word. He wrote to persuade, not to show off, and he mastered that indispensable skill of a popular author: knowing how to clarify complicated issues without yielding to distorting simplifications. His archrival in Washington's administration, Jefferson, paid reluctant tribute to Hamilton's gifts when, in urging Madison to take up his pen to answer Hamilton's newspaper essays, he called him a "mighty host." In the earliest pieces we see the foundations of that brilliant career being set down and the contours of his core commitments established. We can also begin to see how those commitments were gradually adapted to embrace a more energetic vision of government by the time of the Continentalist essays. Understanding something of Hamilton's early writings thus serves to illumine some of the reasons for the earliest political and constitutional controversies of the republic.

Hamilton epitomized what Jefferson feared in Federalist politics. When Hamilton had the chance to draft the economic policy for the nation, he relied on what he called the "durable and permanent existence of rich and poor, debtor and creditor." The wealthy few would develop new enterprises for the poor, whose lives would be regulated through their economic dependence and, if necessary, the master-servant provisions of the Common Law. Convinced of the need for leadership from disinterested and educated gentlemen, Hamilton rejected the notion that ordinary farmers, storekeepers, and tinkerers might just as effectively use their resources for new, unsupervised ventures as wealthy entrepreneurs would. Yet it was the pool of capital and financial stability that Hamilton created that enabled those petty entrepreneurs to prosper when Jefferson became president.

Illustrative of Hamilton's socially conservative attitudes was his reaction to the idea of trade having the capacity of self-regulation. He rejected altogether the existence of a natural social harmony and called Adam Smith's conviction, worked out in *The Wealth of Nations,* that the nation could flourish without "a common directing power," "one of those wild speculative paradoxes, which have grown into credit among us, contrary to the uniform practice and sense of the most enlightened nations."

Like a master technician, Hamilton grasped the impinging details of things as disordered as the mishmash of state and national debts left after eight years of fighting the revolution. Even to speak of debts is to impose a stability on what was in fact a jumble of bonds, bank notes, IOUs, and requisitions of fluctuating value that had passed through hundreds of hands. Only a passion for this kind of fiscal management could entice anyone to take on such a staggering task as registering, calibrating, and streamlining this tangle of papers into a stock issue that would make the United States solvent. With supreme confidence in his proposed measures, Hamilton turned a mass of bad debt into an asset by converting the debt into interest-bearing bonds that people wanted to purchase.

The four geniuses of American nation-building—Jefferson, Hamilton, Madison, and Marshall—found their way unerringly to their métiers: Madison, the constitution writer; Jefferson, the creator of a democratic polity; Marshall, the architect of liberal jurisprudence; and Hamilton, the fiscal wizard. All had interesting relationships with George Washington, whose great virtues were more personal and moral than intellectual. Their writings and stories reflect the character of the nation itself. It's hard not to share the public's delight in learning about them or, as in this case, in reading their own powerful words.

INTRODUCTION

Richard B. Vernier

CONSIDERING THE REPUTATIONS of all the Founding Fathers, that of Alexander Hamilton has taken the wildest swings. Over the past two centuries, he has by turns been vilified as a cunning, aristocratic crypto-monarchist out to strangle American democracy in its cradle, and hailed as a steely-eyed visionary who secured the economic foundations of the republic and fathered the modern American industrial state. How one views Hamilton will necessarily depend upon how one views the great debates of the early republic over the scope and nature of government power, and of its role in shaping American society. Too frequently judgment on these essential questions is formed with reference only to Hamilton's later works, most especially his contributions to the *Federalist Papers*. That is unfortunate, because such a reading necessarily slights the powerful commitment Hamilton made early in his career to the revolutionary cause. Considering his earliest public writings presented in this volume, the most lurid portrayal of Hamilton as hostile to the principles of American republicanism, as an ambitious opportunist who paid lip service to republican government but actively pursued a system of elective monarchy, is unsustainable. Indeed, Hamilton's revolutionary writings reveal the core values and beliefs of a young but genuine Whig. What they suggest is the substitution of a revolutionary's fears for his nation's liberty, with a patriot's desire for his nation's power. To compare *The Farmer Refuted* with *The Continentalist* essays is to be confronted by the very great changes which had taken place in Hamilton's thinking about the challenges confronting American Independence. To compare *The Continentalist* essays with his *Federalist* essays, and even more so his famous state papers on public credit, the bank, and manufactures is to be struck with how much the grand themes sounded there remained central to his subsequent thinking.[1] By collecting his earliest public writings together in one volume, readers will be better able to assess for themselves Hamilton's core commitments and his place in the American political tradition. Did he remain constant in his most basic beliefs, or did he indeed undergo a radical reconsideration of the nature of American political and economic liberty?

The Revolution produced an outpouring of thousands of tracts and newspaper essays, nowhere more ably analyzed and characterized than in Bernard Bailyn's classic *Ideological Origins of the American Revolution.*[2] Hamilton's first tracts, written in the full flush of early Revolutionary fervor, strike most of the familiar notes of patriotic Whiggism delineated by Bailyn. There is the offhanded appeal to natural-law scholars—"I recommend Grotius, Pufendorf, Locke"—the assertion that government rests upon consent, for the protection of natural rights. Real Whig notions of the grasping designs of power against liberty leave Hamilton convinced that British imperial policy clearly indicates a plot against American liberty, that the "system of slavery" being "fabricated against America" is the "offspring of mature deliberation." And that the ultimate aim of the conspiracy was to fasten upon the colonies the system of heavy taxes and tithes, rule by standing army—in a word, to transform Americans into sheep to be shorn at will for the maintenance of a train of court dependents—is likewise assumed by Hamilton. The profound legalism and constitutionalism of the Revolutionary argument is also brilliantly displayed by the young Hamilton. The central Revolutionary claim that Parliament had no power to tax the colonies, either under the terms of the British constitution, or by the terms of colonial charters, is as ably handled by the teenager's sweeping survey of colonial charters as in Jefferson's *Summary View of the Rights of British America* (1774).

There is another feature of the American Whig Revolutionary ideol-

---

1. See, on this transformation, Forrest McDonald, *Alexander Hamilton* (New York: Norton, 1979).

2. Bernard Bailyn, *Ideological Origins of the American Revolution* (Cambridge, Mass.: Belknap Press of Harvard University Press, 1967).

ogy on display in Hamilton's writing which, I suspect, explains the manifest differences between the Hamilton of *The Farmer Refuted* and the Hamilton of the next two decades. Hamilton's argument is suffused with the conviction that the North American trade is indispensable to the well-being of Britain, and indeed, of the whole empire—that a boycott will produce redress, he announced, is a "near certainty." British power was largely illusory, he assured his readers: while luxury was at a high pitch, the people were impoverished, and the country was loaded with taxes, with a staggering load of debt that would take 112 years to pay. The British would never be so foolish as to attempt to wage a war which would only ruin the colony it sought to hold; but if it did, America could field an army thirty times bigger than any the British might send. Moreover, Hamilton shrewdly predicted, Spain and France would both come to America's aid, guided only by national self-interest.

Sanguine visions of easy triumph soon gave way to "the times that try men's souls." General Howe showed up, not with 15,000 troops, but 32,000, heavy artillery, and a massive naval force. In February of 1778 from Valley Forge, Hamilton wrote bitterly to New York Governor Clinton of the "degeneracy of representation in the great council of America. . . . By injudicious changes and arrangements in the Commissary's department, in the middle of a campaign, they have exposed the army frequently to temporary want, and the danger of a dissolution, from absolute famine. At this very day there are complaints from the whole line, of having been three or four days without provisions; desertions have been immense, and strong features of mutiny begin to show themselves." It was only because the very best men eschewed positions in Congress, for places in state government, that the army was in such distress. "Men have been fonder of the emoluments and conveniences, of being employed at home, and local attachment, falsely operating, has made them more provident for the particular interests of the states to which they belonged, than for the common interests of the confederacy."[3]

3. Alexander Hamilton to George Clinton, February 13, 1778, in Harold Syrett and

The inability of Congress to effectively manage an army in the field because of the centripetal force of state parochialism became Hamilton's *idée fixe,* and the spur to his studies of what effective power would look like. By the last year of his military service, the outlines of Hamilton's vision for the republic could be limned in a series of letters he wrote to James Duane and Robert Morris.[4] Most of the ideas in those letters were developed further in *The Continentalist* essays.

The Revolution, he wrote in 1781, had begun without Americans' having an understanding of a government of the "enlarged kind suited to the government of an independent nation." Revolutionary fear of power had produced a "fatal mistake" in the want of power in Congress. Americans had been blind to the fact that "As too much power leads to despotism, too little leads to anarchy." Indeed, history shows that the want of power at the center also threatened liberty: the jealous rivalry of Greek cities led inexorably to internecine wars and foreign subjugation. This fact augured poorly for the republic, since it was in the nature of confederacies for the federal government to be at a disadvantage to its members, as members habitually favored their partial and parochial interests to the good of the whole. Self-seeking by states under the illusion of safety from European depredation would lead to the emergence of mutually rivalrous confederacies in America, each with its own European ally. Even with the country still at war, Hamilton fumed, the states had been loath to vest Congress with the means to fulfill its immense responsibilities, lulled by the illusion that European loans would obviate the need for Congressional revenues. "We did not consider," Hamilton ruefully reflects, "how difficult it must be to exhaust the resources of a nation circumstanced like that of Great Britain." It was urgent, as general European war loomed, that America quickly give Congress the powers it needed to gain decisive advantages on the battlefield, and to prevent "us from being a conquered people." Congress had to be granted broad

---

Jacob E. Cooke, eds., *Papers of Alexander Hamilton* (New York: Columbia University Press, 1961), 1:425–27.

4. Jacob Ernest Cooke, *Alexander Hamilton* (New York: Scribner's, 1982), 22–26.

tax powers, since "Power, without revenue, in political society is a name." By 1781, Hamilton's view of Britain's public debt has reversed: far from betokening weakness, it is the sign of immense strength, since all countries borrow money to fight war. The size of Britain's debt was merely testimony to its enormous credit-worthiness, and to the need for government in America to embrace policies like a national bank which united "the influence and interest of moneyed men with the resources of government" which alone "can give it that durable and extensive credit of which it stands in need."

Hamilton's revolutionary writings, then, are not only important for illuminating the issues at stake in the break with Britain, but for the course the nation would take in the aftermath of independence. In them he gives a foretaste of what is to come, and why.

Hamilton's place in American history as one of its leading figures is not suggested by the circumstances of his birth and early life. He was born on the tiny sugar island of Nevis in the British West Indies, and even his date of birth is uncertain, either January 11, 1755 (the scholarly consensus) or 1757 (Hamilton's own claim). Because his mother failed to obtain a legal divorce from a previous husband who abandoned her, years after Hamilton was born his parents' marriage was voided. Within a year of learning his wife was a "bigamist," and his offspring "whore children," James Hamilton abandoned the family, and Alexander bore the stigma of illegitimate birth—John Adams privately taunted him as "the bastard brat of a Scotch peddlar" after decades of distinguished national service. Orphaned in 1768 by the death of his mother, Hamilton was sent to work as a clerk in a St. Croix merchant's store. There his intellectual gifts made such an impression that in 1772 his employer, together with a Princeton alumnus, Rev. Hugh Knox, arranged to send him to the mainland to be educated. After little more than a year of formal prefatory schooling, Hamilton forsook Princeton to enter King's College (Columbia University), because it acceded to his plans to fly through his studies at his own frenetic pace. It was as a college sophomore that he wrote *A Full Vindication of the Measures of Congress* and *The Farmer Refuted.*

The outbreak of fighting between colonials and the British army led to Hamilton's quick progression from New York militia artillery officer to General Washington's staff in March of 1777. In that capacity, Hamilton made a favorable impression on the future president, as well as on his future father-in-law, Phillip Schuyler, a wealthy New York landowner and major political figure. His marriage to Elizabeth Schuyler in 1780 provided an entree into the highest levels of New York legal and political circles. More importantly, however, his military career shaped his emergence as a proponent of strong national union under a radically reconfigured government with all of the appurtenances of European nation-states. Despite a crushing burden of official duties, Hamilton in this period undertook a self-directed course of wide reading in political economy, public finance, history, and European politics. He came to view the Continental Congress as fundamentally defective in its ability to fund and administer an army, as well as to guarantee the union of states and the direction of America's place on the world stage. The *Continentalist* essays published after he left service are merely ruminations on subjects which he treated at length during this period in an extensive private correspondence.

In February of 1781 he abruptly left Washington's staff in a fit of pique to seek a battlefield command. He acquitted himself bravely at the Battle of Yorktown, left the army, and began legal studies. With blinding speed, after a mere three months' preparation, he passed the New York Bar exams. By 1782, Hamilton was a practicing lawyer, and was tapped by the New York legislature to serve as a delegate to the Congress. During his months in Congress Hamilton was at the forefront of the struggle to vest the government with an import tax, but the plan was defeated by the opposition of Rhode Island and Virginia. Congress's inability to secure permanent revenues led disgruntled army officers in Newburgh, New York, into a conspiracy to threaten mutiny to force payment of back pay. Although Washington defused that crisis in March 1783, by June angry soldiers surrounded Congress in Philadelphia, demanding back pay. Hamilton and the rest of Congress were forced to retreat to Princeton, New Jersey, when the Pennsylvania assembly refused to use the militia to disperse the soldiers. Soon thereafter, Hamilton quit Congress in disgust, to return to the practice of law in New York.

After several years as a successful attorney in important civil litigation, and a founder of the Bank of New York, Hamilton returned to politics when he was selected as one of New York's delegates to the Annapolis convention of 1786 for consideration of amendments to the Articles of Confederation. Since less than half the states had sent delegates to the convention, Hamilton drafted the Convention's call for a second meeting to be held the following year in Philadelphia. Elected to the New York Assembly from New York City in 1787, he was selected as a delegate to the Philadelphia convention. Hamilton was not among the more influential delegates at the Constitutional Convention. His major contribution, a speech on June 18, 1787, argued that nothing short of total sovereignty in the hands of a national government could prevent eventual disunion. Moreover, he urged, a model for such a national government could be found in Britain's: "the best in the world," he declared, in "his private opinion." He therefore offered a republicanized copy, consisting of lifetime tenure for the indirectly elected executive, and a legislative composed of an indirectly elected upper house with life terms, and a popularly elected lower house of three-year terms.[5] Despite its brazenly Anglophile tone—he admitted it "went beyond the ideas of most members"—the speech seems not to have shocked his colleagues, although they paid no heed to his model, but preferred to overhaul Madison's. At the end of the convention, Hamilton, like most of his colleagues, voted in favor of the Constitution as probably the best frame attainable at the time. Indeed, once the Constitution was signed, Hamilton became devoted to the cause of its becoming the basis of national unity and national power.

A little over a month later Hamilton undertook to defend the Constitution against its New York critics (such as Governor George Clinton

5. James Madison, *Notes of Debates in the Federal Convention of 1787* (Athens: Ohio University Press, 1966), 129–39.

and fellow delegate Robert Yates) by enlisting New York legal eminence John Jay and the brilliant Virginian James Madison to join him in authoring *The Federalist Papers* under the collective *nom de plume* "Publius" (previously employed by Hamilton in a pamphlet reprinted in this collection). Hamilton's first essay, addressed to the citizens of New York, appeared in New York's *Independent Journal* on October 27, 1787. Writing with lightning speed, Hamilton and Madison—Jay was limited by health problems to just four essays—produced two or three articles every week, sometimes with the author finishing an essay as the first pages were set in type. Despite the lack of close editorial collaboration, the eighty-five essays appeared in up to four New York papers over the next ten months, systematically countering the critics of the proposed government, and sketching its superiority over the existing Articles of Confederation. His service to the cause of the Constitution went further than *The Federalist*. As a member of New York's constitutional ratifying convention, Hamilton's pro-Constitution delegates were outnumbered by anti-ratifiers by more than two to one, but there his deft political maneuvering, and impassioned defense of the Constitution's republican character, seem to have helped sway many delegates. There is no question, however, that his resolution at that convention calling for the amendment of a Bill of Rights to the document secured its narrow approval, against what had seemed like hopeless odds.

The newly elected president, George Washington, picked his old *aide de camp* to fill the position of secretary of the treasury, and it was here that he left his most lasting stamp on the republic. The measures he pursued as treasury secretary all aimed at the construction of national unity, and the construction of the instruments of national power sufficient to the needs of a world of nation-states. Thus, in his Report on Credit (1790), he wanted domestic securities paid at face value, despite the fact that most had been obtained at steep discounts. He also proposed that the debts of the states be assumed by the Treasury. In the former case, he aimed at winning moneyed and mercantile wealth to the cause of the new government, to ensure a reliable source of government credit for future exigencies. In both cases the tax requirements of debt service would justify a panoply of federal taxes for a long period of time, thus solidifying the essential powers of the new government. Rather than conceiving of the federal government as a tool to enrich the moneyed men, Hamilton was convinced that their favor, and the nation's credit, were essential "as long as nations in general continue to use it as a resource in war. It is impossible for a country to contend, on equal terms, or to be secure against the enterprises of other nations, without being able equally with them to avail itself of this important resource."[6]

The Bank of the United States, for all that Hamilton's Report portrayed its benefits to commerce in general, was first and foremost an adjunct of federal finance: by 1796, more than 60 percent of its capital had been loaned to the government.[7] And his defense of its constitutionality, which marked the appearance of his doctrine of implied powers, was perfectly congruent with his previous claim that "there is no rule by which we can measure the momentum of civil power, necessary" and that the union must therefore "possess all the means and have a right to resort to all the methods with which it is entrusted."[8] His Report on Manufactures explicitly endorsed their promotion by the government to "render the United States independent of foreign nations for military and other essential supplies." By this Hamilton meant more than cannon and musket works; he meant "the means of subsistence, habitation, clothing, and defense." "The extreme embarrassments of the United States during the late war," he reminded his countrymen, "from an incapacity of supplying themselves, are still a matter of keen recollection; a future war might be expected again to exemplify the mischiefs and dangers of a

6. Alexander Hamilton, "Second Report on Public Credit" (December 1794), in Henry C. Lodge, ed., *Works of Alexander Hamilton* (New York and London: G. P. Putnam's Sons, 1904), 295–96.

7. Edwin J. Perkins, *American Public Finance and Financial Services, 1700–1815* (Columbus: Ohio State University Press, 1994), 240–44.

8. Alexander Hamilton, "Federalist Papers," quoted in Cooke, *Alexander Hamilton*, 57.

situation to which that incapacity is still, in too great a degree, applicable, unless changed by timely and vigorous exertion."[9]

The effect of these policies, and their rationales, upon the young nation was to create deep divisions between those who saw them as essential and those who saw them as irrelevant, indeed, inimical to the emergence of a free social order. Hamilton's vision of national strength depended above all on the endless attentions and devotions of statesmen to actively design and execute the nation's interest. Nowhere is this clearer than in his argument in *Continentalist* V that among the powers that Congress had to obtain were broad powers to regulate economic activity for the common good. Indeed, Britain's prosperity was the consequence of the growth of its trade, which was due to "the fostering care of government" beginning in the reign of Elizabeth. His Democratic Republican opponents, seeing what he wrought to make the nation strong, complained he was re-creating the very European models the Revolution had fled. On his return from Europe, one writer expressed his "mortification" that as European nations were "sick at length at their enormous and perpetual taxes, and struggling to get rid of them . . . I find we are pursuing the mad policy of increasing and perpetuating both." Similarly, just when European nations were finally learning "to unshackle commerce . . . from excessive burdens and galling restrictions," America was busy "overloading it with duties, and forcing ourselves into impolitic regulations."[10]

By 1792 the divisions had hardened to the point that a newspaper duel of polemics occurred between essays appearing in the Hamilton-backed *Gazette of the United States,* and the Jefferson and Madison–created *National Gazette.* The French Revolution, and the outbreak of war in Europe, inflamed partisan divisions in America to a fever pitch, with Fed-

9. Alexander Hamilton, "Report on Manufactures," in Samuel McKee Jr., ed., *Papers on Public Credit, Commerce, and Finance, by Alexander Hamilton* (New York: Columbia University Press, 1934), 70, 135–36.

10. "Observations on the present state of affairs . . . ," *American Museum* (August 1792), 108–9.

eralists seeing their Republican adversaries as incipient Jacobins, and Republicans viewing the Federalist administration as toadies of the British. Hamilton stepped into the fray with gusto, writing tracts defending abrogation of the treaty with France, calling for the suppression of whiskey tax rebels, and arguing that the deeply unpopular treaty with Britain negotiated by John Jay was in fact the best deal which prudence allowed. Hamilton retired from office at the start of 1795, but continued to be at the center of the polemical warfare that grew increasingly shrill in the last years of the eighteenth century. He was by far the most prolific pamphleteer of all the Founding Fathers. Unfortunately for his political career, he employed his pen in the last years of Adams's presidency in splenetic attacks on the leader of his party. The Republicans won victory in the presidential election of 1800, but produced a tie between Jefferson and Burr which threw the election into the House of Representatives. Hamilton now turned his venom on Burr, whom he reviled in a letter-writing campaign to House members as an unscrupulous, dangerous Catiline. Jefferson won. It was Hamilton's last service to the republic. In 1804, the bad blood between the two stirred mysteriously again, and Burr shot him dead in a duel in New Jersey.

HAMILTON CHRONOLOGY

Jan. 11, 1757	Alexander Hamilton born in the island of Nevis.
Oct., 1772	Arrives in New York.
1773	Enters college.
Dec. 15, 1774	Publishes the *Full Vindication*.
1775	Joins a volunteer corps.
1776	Takes command of artillery company.
March 1, 1777	Joins Washington's Staff.
1779	Writes his first letter to Robert Morris on the National Bank.
Sept. 3, 1780	Letter to Duane on Government.
Dec. 14, 1780	Married to Miss Schuyler.
1782	Admitted to the bar.
June, 1782	Appointed Receiver of Taxes.
Nov., 1782	Enters Congress.
1783	Returns to practice of the law.
1786	Delegate to Annapolis Convention.
1786	Elected to the New York Legislature.
1787	Delegate to the Philadelphia Convention.
1787	Writes the *Federalist*.
1788	Delegate to the New York Convention.
Sept., 1789	Appointed Secretary of the Treasury.
Jan. 14, 1790	Transmits to the House the First Report on the Public Credit.
Jan. 31, 1795	Resigns the Secretaryship of the Treasury and returns to the practice of the law.
July 25, 1798	Appointed Inspector-General of the Army with the rank of Major-General.

July 2, 1800	Retires from the army.
July 11, 1804	Shot by Burr in a duel at Weehawken.
July 12, 1804	Death.

A FULL VINDICATION

OF THE

Measures of Congress from the calumnies of their enemies, in answer to a letter under the signature of a Westchester Farmer; whereby his *sophistry* is exposed, his *cavils* confuted, his *artifices* detected, and his *wit* ridiculed, in a General Address to the inhabitants of America, and a Particular Address to the Farmers of the *Province of New York*. Veritas magna est et prevalebit—Truth is powerful and will prevail. New York: printed by James Rivington: 1774.

ON OCTOBER 14, 1774, the Continental Congress issued its Declaration and Resolves in response to Parliament's legislative retaliation for the Boston Tea Party. The Coercive Acts, as they came to be called, were four-fold: The Boston Port Act shut the Boston Harbor to all ocean traffic; the second act made the Massachusetts Council appointive and limited town meetings; the third allowed royal officials charged with capital crimes in the colonies to be tried in England; and the fourth authorized the quartering of troops in Massachusetts homes. The Congressional Resolves affirmed colonial rights to life, liberty, and property; the right of "all natural-born subjects within the Realm of England" to participate in legislation; the inability of Parliament to represent the colonies; and the sanctity of immunities and privileges bestowed by royal charters or provincial laws. Americans would not submit to violations of their rights, the Congress declared, and would, in response, enter into a "nonimportation, nonconsumption, and nonexportation agreement or association."

The Reverend Samuel Seabury, an Anglican priest in Westchester, New York, using the pseudonym "A Westchester Farmer" (a dig at the famed patriot pamphleteer of the previous decade "A Pennsylvania Farmer"), published an attack on the Congressional Resolves. It appeared first in James Rivington's newspaper, the *New York Gazeteer*, and later was republished as a pamphlet, *Free Thoughts on the Proceedings of the*

Continental Congress (New York, 1774). Castigating the nonimportation association as a "brood of scorpions," he charged Congress with acting illegally, recklessly exposing farmers to economic ruin, and the colonies to the threat of war. Seabury's arguments were widely seen as a blow to the patriot cause.

Alexander Hamilton had recently entered King's College in New York City. The president of the college, Dr. Myles Cooper, himself an Anglican, was an ardent Loyalist, as was a sizable portion of the city. Notwithstanding his tutelage by Dr. Cooper, Hamilton had by the summer of 1774 begun to speak at the liberty pole erected by the New York Sons of Liberty and published his response to Seabury on December 15, 1774.*

---

* A liberty pole was a large wooden pole, stuck in the ground, to provide a meeting point to air complaints about government policy. The tradition goes back to England, but New York's liberty poles (a red flag announced that a meeting of the Sons of Liberty was to be held) date to one erected in 1766 to celebrate the withdrawal of the Stamp Act taxes. Throughout the Revolutionary era, pitched battles were sometimes fought as colonial officials endeavored to tear them down, and revolutionary groups restored them. See J. R. Pole and Jack Greene, eds., *A Companion to the American Revolution* (Oxford, 2003), 155.

A FULL VINDICATION

December 15, 1774.

FRIENDS AND COUNTRYMEN:

It was hardly to be expected that any man could be so presumptuous as openly to controvert the equity, wisdom, and authority of the measures adopted by the Congress—an assembly truly respectable on every ac-count, whether we consider the characters of the men who composed it, the number and dignity of their constituents, or the important ends for which they were appointed. But, however improbable such a degree of presumption might have seemed, we find there are some in whom it exists. Attempts are daily making to diminish the influence of their de-cisions, and prevent the salutary effects intended by them. The impotence of such insidious efforts is evident from the general indignation they are treated with; so that no material ill-consequences can be dreaded from them. But lest they should have a tendency to mislead, and prejudice the minds of a few, it cannot be deemed altogether useless to bestow some notice upon them.

And first, let me ask these restless spirits, Whence arises that violent antipathy they seem to entertain, not only to the natural rights of man-kind, but to common-sense and common modesty? That they are ene-mies to the natural rights of mankind is manifest, because they wish to see one part of their species enslaved by another. That they have an invincible aversion to common-sense is apparent in many respects: they endeavor to persuade us that the absolute sovereignty of Parliament does not imply our absolute slavery; that it is a Christian duty to submit to be plundered of all we have, merely because some of our fellow-subjects are wicked enough to require it of us; that slavery, so far from being a great evil, is a great blessing; and even that our contest with Britain is founded entirely upon the petty duty of three pence per pound on East India tea, whereas the whole world knows it is built upon this interesting question, whether the inhabitants of Great Britain have a right to dispose of the lives and properties of the inhabitants of America, or not. And lastly, that these men have discarded all pretension to common modesty, is clear from hence: first, because they, in the plainest terms, call an august body of men, famed for their patriotism and abilities, fools or knaves; and of course the people whom they represented cannot be exempt from the same opprobrious appellations; and secondly, because they set themselves up as standards of wisdom and probity, by contradicting and censuring the public voice in favor of those men.

A little consideration will convince us that the Congress, instead of having "ignorantly misunderstood, carelessly neglected, or basely betrayed the interests of the colonies," have, on the contrary, devised and recommended the only effectual means to secure the freedom, and establish the future prosperity of America upon a solid basis. If we are not free and happy hereafter, it must proceed from the want of integrity and resolution in executing what they have concerted, not from the temerity or impolicy of their determinations.

Before I proceed to confirm this assertion by the most obvious arguments, I will premise a few brief remarks. The only distinction between freedom and slavery consists in this: In the former state a man is governed by the laws to which he has given his consent, either in person or by his representative; in the latter, he is governed by the will of another. In the one case, his life and property are his own; in the other, they depend upon the pleasure of his master. It is easy to discern which of these two states is preferable. No man in his senses can hesitate in choosing to be free, rather than a slave.

That Americans are entitled to freedom is incontestable on every rational principle. All men have one common original: they participate in one common nature, and consequently have one common right. No reason can be assigned why one man should exercise any power or preeminence over his fellow-creatures more than another; unless they have voluntarily vested him with it. Since, then, Americans have not, by any act of theirs, empowered the British Parliament to make laws for them, it follows they can have no just authority to do it.

Besides the clear voice of natural justice in this respect, the fundamental principles of the English constitution are in our favor. It has been repeatedly demonstrated that the idea of legislation or taxation, when the subject is not represented, is inconsistent with *that*. Nor is this all; our charters, the express conditions on which our progenitors relinquished their native countries, and came to settle in this, preclude every claim of ruling and taxing us without our assent.

Every subterfuge that sophistry has been able to invent, to evade or obscure this truth, has been refuted by the most conclusive reasonings; so that we may pronounce it a matter of undeniable certainty, that the pretensions of Parliament are contradictory to the law of nature, subversive of the British constitution, and destructive of the faith of the most solemn compacts.

What, then, is the subject of our controversy with the mother country? It is this: Whether we shall preserve that security to our lives and properties, which the law of nature, the genius of the British constitution, and our charters, afford us; or whether we shall resign them into the hands of the British House of Commons, which is no more privileged to dispose of them than the Great Mogul. What can actuate those men who labor to delude any of us into an opinion that the object of contention between the parent state and the colonies is only three pence duty upon tea; or that the commotions in America originate in a plan, formed by some turbulent men, to erect it into a republican government? The Parliament claims a right to tax us in all cases whatsoever; its late acts* are in virtue of that claim. How ridiculous, then, is it to affirm that we

---

* The "late acts" referred to here are Parliament's repeated affirmations of its 1766 Declaratory Act, which insisted that the repeal of colonial Stamp Act duties was purely expedient and that Parliament maintained the power to legislate for the colonies "in all Cases whatsoever."

are quarrelling for the trifling sum of three pence a pound on tea, when it is evidently the principle against which we contend.

The design of electing members to represent us in general Congress was, that the wisdom of America might be collected in devising the most proper and expedient means to repel this atrocious invasion of our rights. It has been accordingly done. Their decrees are binding upon all, and demand a religious observance.

We did not, especially in this province, circumscribe them by any fixed boundary; and therefore, as they cannot be said to have exceeded the limits of their authority, their act must be esteemed the act of their constituents. If it should be objected that they have not answered the end of their election, but have fallen upon an improper and ruinous mode of proceeding, I reply by asking, Who shall be the judge? Shall any individual oppose his private sentiment to the united counsels of men in whom America has reposed so high a confidence? The attempt must argue no small degree of arrogance and self-sufficiency.

Yet this attempt has been made; and it is become, in some measure, necessary to vindicate the conduct of this venerable assembly from the aspersions of men who are their adversaries only because they are foes to America.

When the political salvation of any community is depending, it is incumbent upon those who are set up as its guardians to embrace such measures as have justice, vigor, and a probability of success to recommend them. If, instead of this, they take those methods which are in themselves feeble and little likely to succeed, and may, through a defect in vigor, involve the community in a still greater danger, they may be justly considered as its betrayers. It is not enough, in times of imminent peril, to use only possible means of preservation. Justice and sound policy dictate the use of probable means.

The only scheme of opposition suggested by those who have been and are averse from a non-importation and non-exportation agreement, is by REMONSTRANCE and PETITION. The authors and abettors of this scheme have never been able to invent a single argument to prove the likelihood of its succeeding. On the other hand, there are many standing facts and valid considerations against it.

In the infancy of the present dispute, we had recourse to this method only. We addressed the throne in the most loyal and respectful manner, in a legislative capacity; but what was the consequence? Our address was treated with contempt and neglect. The first American Congress did the same, and met with similar treatment. The total repeal of the stamp act, and the partial repeal of the revenue acts, took place not because the complaints of America were deemed just and reasonable, but because these acts were found to militate against the commercial interests of Great Britain. This was the declared motive of the repeal.

These instances are sufficient for our purpose; but they derive greater validity and force from the following:

The legal assembly of Massachusetts Bay presented, not long since, a most humble, dutiful, and earnest petition to his Majesty, requesting the dismission of a governor highly odious to the people, and whose misrepresentations they regarded as one chief source of all their calamities. Did they succeed in their request? No—it was treated with the greatest indignity, and stigmatized as "a seditious, vexatious, and scandalous libel."

I know the men I have to deal with will acquiesce in this stigma. Will they also dare to calumniate the noble and spirited petition that came from the Mayor and Aldermen of the city of London? Will they venture to justify the unparalleled stride of power by which Popery and arbitrary dominion were established in Canada? The citizens of London remonstrated against it; they signified its repugnancy to the principles of the revolution; but, like ours, their complaints were unattended to. From thence we may learn how little dependence ought to be placed on this method of obtaining the redress of grievances.

There is less reason now than ever to expect deliverance, in this way, from the hand of oppression. The system of slavery, fabricated against America, cannot, at this time, be considered as the effect of inconsideration and rashness. It is the offspring of mature deliberation. It has been fostered by time and strengthened by every artifice human subtility is capable of. After the claims of Parliament had lain dormant for a while, they are again resumed and prosecuted with more than common ardor. The Premier has advanced too far to recede with safety. He is deeply interested to execute his purpose, if possible. We know he has declared that he will never desist till he has brought America to his feet; and we may conclude nothing but necessity will induce him to abandon his aims. In common life, to retract an error, even in the beginning, is no easy task; perseverance confirms us in it, and rivets the difficulty. But in a public station, to have been in an error and to have persisted in it when it is detected, ruins both reputation and fortune. To this we may add, that disappointment and opposition inflame the minds of men and attach them still more to their mistakes.

What can we represent which has not already been represented? What petitions can we offer that have not already been offered? The rights of America and the injustice of Parliamentary pretensions have been clearly and repeatedly stated, both in and out of Parliament. No new arguments can be framed to operate in our favor. Should we even resolve the errors of the Ministry and Parliament into the fallibility of human understanding, if they have not yet been convinced we have no prospect of being able to do it by anything further we can say. But if we impute their conduct to a wicked thirst of domination and disregard to justice, we have no hope of prevailing with them to alter it by expatiating on our rights and suing to their compassion for relief; especially since we have found, by various experiments, the inefficacy of such methods. Upon the whole, it is morally certain this mode of opposition would be fruitless and defective. The exigency of the times requires vigorous and probable remedies; not weak and improbable. It would, therefore, be the extreme of folly to place any confidence in, much less confine ourselves wholly to, it.

This being the case, we can have no resource but in a restriction of our trade, or in a resistance *vi et armis*. It is impossible to conceive any other alternative. Our Congress, therefore, have imposed what restraint they thought necessary. Those who condemn or clamor against it do nothing more nor less than advise us to be slaves.

I shall now examine the principal measures of the Congress, and vindicate them fully from the charge of injustice or impolicy.

Were I to argue in a philosophical manner, I might say the obligation to a mutual intercourse in the way of trade, with the inhabitants of Great Britain, Ireland, and the West Indies, is of the *imperfect* kind. There is no law, either of nature or of the civil society in which we live, that obliges us to purchase and make use of the products and manufactures of a different land or people. It is indeed a dictate of humanity to contribute to the support and happiness of our fellow-creatures, and more especially those who are allied to us by the ties of blood, interest, and mutual protection; but humanity does not require us to sacrifice our own security and welfare to the convenience or advantage of others. Self-preservation is the first principle of our nature. When our lives and properties are at stake, it would be foolish and unnatural to refrain from such measures as might preserve them because they would be detrimental to others.

But we are justified upon another principle besides this. Though the manufacturers of Great Britain and Ireland and the inhabitants of the West Indies are not chargeable with any actual crime toward America, they may, in a political view, be esteemed criminal. In a civil society it is the duty of each particular branch to promote not only the good of the whole community, but the good of every other particular branch. If one part endeavors to violate the rights of another, the rest ought to assist in preventing the injury. When they do not but remain neutral, they are deficient in their duty, and may be regarded, in some measure, as accomplices.

The reason of this is obvious from the design of civil society; which is, that the united strength of the several members might give stability and security to the whole body, and each respective member; so that one part cannot encroach upon another without becoming a common enemy, and eventually endangering the safety and happiness of all the other parts.

Since, then, the persons who will be distressed by the methods we are using for our own protection, have, by their neutrality, first committed a breach of an obligation similar to that which bound us to consult their emolument, it is plain the obligation upon us is annulled, and we are blameless in what we are about to do.

With respect to the manufacturers of Great Britain, they are criminal in a more particular sense. Our oppression arises from that member of the great body politic of which they compose a considerable part. So far as their influence has been wanting to counteract the iniquity of their rulers, so far they acquiesced in it, and are deemed to be confederates in their guilt. It is impossible to exculpate a people that suffers its rulers to abuse and tyrannize over others.

It may not be amiss to add, that we are ready to receive with open arms any who may be sufferers by the operation of our measures, and recompense them with every blessing our country affords to honest industry. We will receive them as brethren, and make them sharers with us in all the advantages we are struggling for.

From these plain and indisputable principles, the mode of opposition we have chosen is reconcilable to the strictest maxims of justice. It remains now to be examined whether it has also the sanction of good policy.

To render it agreeable to good policy, three things are requisite. First, that the necessity of the times requires it; secondly, that it be not the probable source of greater evils than those it pretends to remedy; and lastly, that it have a probability of success.

That the necessity of the times demands it, needs but little elucidation. We are threatened with absolute slavery. It has been proved that resistance by means of REMONSTRANCE and PETITION would not be efficacious, and, of course, that a restriction on our trade is the only peaceable method in our power to avoid the impending mischief. It follows, therefore, that such a restriction is necessary.

That it is not the probable source of greater evils than those it pretends to remedy, may easily be determined. The most abject slavery, which comprehends almost every species of human misery, is what it is designed to prevent.

The consequences of the means are a temporary stagnation of commerce, and thereby a deprivation of the luxuries and some of the conveniences of life. The necessaries and many of the conveniences our own fertile and propitious soil affords us.

No person that has enjoyed the sweets of liberty can be insensible of its infinite value, or can reflect on its reverse without horror and detestation. No person that is not lost to every generous feeling of humanity, or that is not stupidly blind to his own interest, could bear to offer himself and posterity as victims at the shrine of despotism, in preference to enduring the shortlived inconveniences that may result from an abridgment, or even entire suspension, of commerce.

Were not the disadvantages of slavery too obvious to stand in need of it, I might enumerate and describe the tedious train of calamities inseparable from it. I might show that it is fatal to religion and morality; that it tends to debase the mind, and corrupt its noblest springs of action. I might show that it relaxes the sinews of industry, clips the wings of commerce, and introduces misery and indigence in every shape.

Under the auspices of tyranny the life of the subject is often sported with, and the fruits of his daily toil are consumed in oppressive taxes, that serve to gratify the ambition, avarice, and lusts of his superiors. Every court minion riots in the spoils of the honest laborer, and despises the hand by which he is fed. The page of history is replete with instances that loudly warn us to beware of slavery.

ROME was the nurse of freedom. She was celebrated for her justice and lenity; but in what manner did she govern her dependent provinces? They were made the continual scene of rapine and cruelty. From thence let us learn how little confidence is due to the wisdom and equity of the most exemplary nations.

Should Americans submit to become the vassals of their fellow-subjects in Great Britain, their yoke will be peculiarly grievous and intolerable. A vast majority of mankind is entirely biassed by motives of self-interest. Most men are glad to remove any burthens off themselves, and place them upon the necks of their neighbors. We cannot, therefore, doubt but that the British Parliament, with a view to the ease and advantage of itself and its constituents, would oppress and grind the Americans as much as possible. Jealousy would concur with selfishness; and for fear of the future independence of America, if it should be permitted to rise to too great a height of splendor and opulence, every method would be taken to drain it of its wealth and restrain its prosperity. We are already suspected of aiming at independence, and that is one principal cause of the severity we experience. The same cause will always operate against us, and produce a uniform severity of treatment.

The evils which may flow from the execution of our measures, if we consider them with respect to their extent and duration, are comparatively nothing. In all human probability they will scarcely be felt. Reason and experience teach us that the consequences would be too fatal to Great Britain to admit of delay. There is an immense trade between her and the colonies. The revenues arising from thence are prodigious. The consumption of her manufactures in these colonies supplies the means of subsistence to a vast number of her most useful inhabitants. The experiment we have made heretofore shows us of how much importance our commercial connection is to her, and gives us the highest assurance of obtaining immediate redress by suspending it.

From these considerations it is evident she must do something decisive. She must either listen to our complaints and restore us to a peaceful enjoyment of our violated rights, or she must exert herself to enforce her despotic claims by fire and sword. To imagine she would prefer the latter, implies a charge of the grossest infatuation, of madness itself. Our numbers are very considerable; the courage of Americans has been tried and proved. Contests for liberty have ever been found the most bloody, implacable, and obstinate. The disciplined troops Great Britain could send against us would be but few. Our superiority in number would overbalance our inferiority in discipline. It would be a hard, if not impracticable, task to subjugate us by force.

Besides, while Great Britain was engaged in carrying on an unnatural war against us, her commerce would be in a state of decay. Her revenues would be decreasing. An armament, sufficient to enslave America, would put her to an insupportable expense.

She would be laid open to the attacks of foreign enemies. Ruin, like a deluge, would pour in from every quarter. After lavishing her blood and treasure to reduce us to a state of vassalage, she would herself become a prey to some triumphant neighbor.

These are not imaginary mischiefs. The colonies contain above three millions of people. Commerce flourishes with the most rapid progress throughout them. This commerce Great Britain has hitherto regulated to her own advantage. Can we think the annihilation of so exuberant a source of wealth a matter of trifling import? On the contrary, must it not be productive of the most disastrous effects? It is evident it must. It is equally evident, that the conquest of so numerous a people, armed in the animating cause of liberty, could not be accomplished without an inconceivable expense of blood and treasure.

We cannot, therefore, suspect Great Britain to be capable of such frantic extravagance as to hazard these dreadful consequences; without which, she must necessarily desist from her unjust pretensions, and leave us in the undisturbed possession of our privileges.

Those who affect to ridicule the resistance America might make to the military force of Great Britain, and represent its humiliation as a matter the most easily to be achieved, betray either a mind clouded by the most irrational prejudices, or a total ignorance of human nature. However, it must be the wish of every honest man never to see a trial.

But should we admit a possibility of a third course, as our pamphleteer supposes—that is, the endeavoring to bring us to a compliance by putting a stop to our whole trade, even this would not be so terrible as he pretends. We can live without trade of any kind. Food and clothing we have within ourselves. Our climate produces cotton, wool, flax, and hemp; which, with proper cultivation, would furnish us with summer apparel in abundance. The article of cotton, indeed, would do more; it would contribute to defend us from the inclemency of winter. We have sheep, which, with due care in improving and increasing them, would soon yield a sufficiency of wool. The large quantity of skins we have among us would never let us want a warm and comfortable suit. It would be no unbecoming employment for our daughters to provide silks of their own country. The silk-worm answers as well here as in any part of the world. Those hands which may be deprived of business by the cessation of commerce, may be occupied in various kinds of manufactures and other internal improvements. If, by the necessity of the thing, manufactures should once be established, and take root among us, they will pave the way still more to the future grandeur and glory of America; and, by lessening its need of external commerce, will render it still securer against the encroachments of tyranny.

It is, however, chimerical to imagine, that the circumstances of Great Britain will admit of such a tardy method of subjugating us, for reasons which have been already given, and which shall be corroborated by others equally forcible.

I come now to consider the last and principal ingredient that constitutes the policy of a measure, which is, a probability of success. I have been obliged to anticipate this part of my subject in considering the second requisite; and, indeed, what I have already said seems to me to leave no room for doubting that the means we have used will be successful; but I shall here examine the matter more thoroughly, and endeavor to evince it more fully.

The design of the Congress in their proceedings, it cannot and need not be denied, was, either, by a prospect of the evil consequences, to influence the ministry to give up their enterprise, or, should they prove inflexible, to affect the inhabitants of Great Britain, Ireland, and the West Indies in such a manner as to rouse them from their state of neutrality, and engage them to unite with us in opposing the lawless hand of tyranny, which is extended to ravish our liberty from us, and might soon be extended for the same purpose against them.

The FARMER mentions, as one probable consequence of our measures, "clamors, discord, confusion, mobs, riots, insurrections, rebellions in Great Britain, Ireland, and the West Indies"; though at the same time he thinks *it is,* he also thinks *it is not,* a probable consequence. For my part, without hazarding any such seeming contradictions, I shall, in a plain way, assert that I verily believe a non-importation and a non-exportation will effect all the purposes they are intended for.

It is no easy matter to make any tolerably exact estimate of the advantages that accrue to Great Britain, Ireland, and the West Indies from their commercial intercourse with the colonies; nor, indeed, is it necessary. Every man, the least acquainted with the state and extent of our trade, must be convinced it is the source of immense revenues to the parent state, and gives employment and bread to a vast number of his Majesty's subjects. It is impossible but that a suspension of it, for any time, must introduce beggary and wretchedness, in an eminent degree, both in England and Ireland. And as to the West India plantations, they could not possibly subsist without us. I am the more confident of this, because I have a pretty general acquaintance with their circumstances and dependencies.

We are told, "that it is highly improbable we shall succeed in distressing the people of Great Britain, Ireland, and the West Indies so far as to oblige them to join with us in getting the acts of Parliament which we complain of repealed. The first distress," it is said, "will fall on ourselves; it will be more severely felt by us than any part of his Majesty's dominions, and will affect us the longest. The fleets of Great Britain command respect throughout the globe. Her influence extends to every part of the earth. Her manufactures are equal to any, superior to most, in the world. Her wealth is great. Her people enterprising and persevering in their attempts to extend, and enlarge, and protect her trade. The total loss of our trade will be felt only for a time. Her merchants would turn their attention another way; new sources of trade and wealth would be opened; new schemes pursued. She would soon find a vent for all her manufactures in spite of all we could do. Our malice would hurt only ourselves. Should our schemes distress some branches of her trade, it would be only for a time; and there is ability and humanity enough in the nation to relieve those that are distressed by us, and put them in some other way of getting their living."

The omnipotency and all-sufficiency of Great Britain may be pretty good topics for her passionate admirers to exercise their declamatory powers upon, for amusement and trial of skill; but they ought not to be proposed to the world as matters of truth and reality. In the calm, unprejudiced eye of reason, they are altogether visionary. As to her wealth, it is notorious that she is oppressed with a heavy national debt, which it requires the utmost policy and economy ever to discharge. Luxury has arrived to a great pitch; and it is a universal maxim, that luxury indicates the declension of a state. Her subjects are loaded with the most enormous taxes. All circumstances agree in declaring their distress. The continual emigrations from Great Britain and Ireland to the continent are a glaring symptom that those kingdoms are a good deal impoverished.

The attention of Great Britain has hitherto been constantly awake to expand her commerce. She has been vigilant to explore every region with which it might be her interest to trade. One of the principal branches of her commerce is with the colonies. These colonies, as they are now settled and peopled, have been the work of near two centuries. They are blessed with every advantage of soil, climate, and situation. They have advanced with an almost incredible rapidity. It is, therefore, an egregious piece of absurdity to affirm, that the loss of our trade would be felt for a time (which must only signify for a short time). No new schemes could be pursued that would not require, at least, as much time to repair the loss of our trade, as was spent in bringing it to its present degree of perfection, which is near two centuries. Nor can it be reasonably imagined, that the total and sudden loss of so extensive and lucrative a branch would not produce the most violent effects to a nation that subsists entirely upon its commerce.

It is said "there is ability and humanity enough in the nation to relieve those who are distressed by us, and to put them into some other way of getting their living." I wish the gentleman had obliged his readers so much as to have pointed out this other way. I must confess, I have racked my brains to no purpose to discover it; and I am fully of opinion it is purely ideal. Besides the common mechanic arts, which are subservient to the ordinary uses of life, and which are the instruments of commerce, I know no other ways, in time of peace, in which men can be employed, except in agriculture and the liberal arts. Persons employed in the mechanic arts are those whom the abridgment of commerce would immediately affect; and as to such branches as might be less affected, they are already sufficiently stocked with workmen, and could give bread to no more. Not only so, but I can't see by what legerdemain a weaver, a clothier, could be at once converted into a carpenter or blacksmith. With respect to agriculture, the lands of Great Britain and Ireland have been long ago distributed and taken up; nor do they require any additional laborers to till them, so that there could be no employment in this way. The liberal arts cannot maintain those who are already devoted to them; not to say, it is more than probable, the generality of mechanics would make but indifferent philosophers, poets, painters, and musicians.

What poor shifts is sophistry obliged to have recourse to! We are threatened with the resentment of those against whom our measures will operate. It is said that "instead of conciliating we shall alienate the affections of the people of Great Britain; of friends, we shall make them our enemies." And further, that "we shall excite the resentment of the government at home against us, which will do us no good, but, on the contrary, much harm."

Soon after we are told that "we shall probably raise the resentment of the Irish and West Indians. The passions of human nature," it is said, "are much the same in all countries. If they find us disposed wantonly to distress them, to serve our own purposes, they will look out for some method to do without us. Will they not look elsewhere for a supply of those articles they used to take from us? They would deserve to be despised for their meanness, did they not."

To these objections I reply, first, with respect to the inhabitants of

Great Britain: that if they are our friends, as is supposed, and as we have reason to believe, they cannot, without being destitute of rationality, be incensed against us for using the only peaceable and probable means in our power to preserve our invaded rights. They know, by their own experience, how fruitless remonstrances and petitions are. They know we have tried them, over and over, to no purpose. They know also how dangerous to their liberties the loss of ours must be. What, then, could excite their resentment, if they have the least regard to common justice? The calamities that threaten them proceed from the weakness or wickedness of their own rulers, which compels us to take the measures we do. The insinuation, that we *wantonly* distress them to serve our own purposes, is futile, and unsupported by a single argument. I have shown we could have no other resource; nor can they think our conduct such, without a degree of infatuation that it would be impossible to provide against, and therefore useless to consult. It is most reasonable to believe they will revenge the evils they may feel, on the true authors of them—on an aspiring and ill-judged ministry; not on us who act out of a melancholy necessity, and are the innocent causes in self-defence.

With respect to the ministry, it is certain that any thing which has a tendency to frustrate their designs will not fail to excite their displeasure. But since we have nothing to expect from their justice and lenity, it can be no objection to a measure that it tends to stir up their resentment. But their resentment (it is often said) may ruin us. The impossibility of doing that, without at the same time ruining Great Britain, is a sufficient security.

The same may be said with regard to the Irish and the West Indians, which has been said concerning the people of Great Britain. The Irish, in particular, by their own circumstances, will be taught to sympathize with us, and commend our conduct. Justice will direct their resentment to its proper objects.

It is true, self-love will prompt both the Irish and the West Indians to take every method in their power to escape the miseries they are in danger of. But what methods can they take? "The Irish," it is said, "may be supplied with flax-seed from Holland, the Baltic, and the river St.

Lawrence. Canada produces no inconsiderable quantity already." And as to the West Indies, "they produce now many of the necessaries of life. The quantity may be easily increased. Canada will furnish them with many articles they now take from us: flour, lumber, horses, etc. Georgia, the Floridas, and the Mississippi abound in lumber; Nova Scotia, in fish."

The Dutch are rivals to the English in their commerce. They make large quantities of fine linens, gauze, laces, etc., which require the flax to be picked before it comes to seed; for which reason, it is not in their power to raise much more seed than they want for their own use. Ireland has always had the surplus from them. They could, if they were ever so willing, enlarge their usual supplies but very little. It is, indeed, probable they may withhold them. They may choose to improve the occasion for the advancement of their own trade. They may take advantage of the scarcity of materials in Ireland, to increase and put off their own manufactures.

The Baltic has ever supplied Ireland with its flax; and she has been able to consume that, with all she could derive from other quarters.

As to Canada, I am well informed, it could at present afford but a very inconsiderable quantity. It has had little encouragement, hitherto, to raise that article; and, of course, has not much attended to it. The instances mentioned of seed being "bought up there at a low price, brought to New York, and sold to the Irish factors at a great advance," does not prove there is any quantity raised there. Its cheapness proceeds from there being no demand for it; and where there was no demand, there was no inducement to cultivate it.

Upon the whole, it appears that the supplies of flax-seed which Ireland might draw elsewhere would be trifling, in comparison with those received from us, and not at all equivalent to her wants. But if this were not the case, if she might procure a sufficiency without our help, yet could she not do without us. She would want purchasers for her linens after they were manufactured; and where could she find any so numerous and wealthy as we are? I must refer it to the profound sagacity of Mr. A. W. Farmer to explore them. It is too arduous a task for me.

Much less could the West Indies subsist independent of us. Notwithstanding the continual imports from hence, there is seldom, or never, in any of the islands, a sufficient stock of provisions to last six months, which may give us an idea how great the consumption is. The necessaries they produce within themselves, when compared with the consumption, are scarcely worth mentioning. Very small portions of the land are appropriated to the production of such necessaries; indeed, it is too valuable to admit of it. Nor could the quantity be increased to any material degree, without applying the whole of the land to it. It is alleged that "Canada will furnish them with flour, lumber, horses, etc.," and that "Georgia, the Floridas, and Mississippi abound in lumber; Nova Scotia, in fish." These countries have been all along carrying on a trade to the West Indies as well as we; and can it be imagined that, alone, they will be able to supply them tolerably? The Canadians have been indolent, and have not improved their country as they ought to have done. The wheat they raise at present, over and above what they have occasion for themselves, would be found to go but little way among the islands. Those who think the contrary, must have mistaken notions of them. They must be unapprised of the number of souls they contain. Almost every one hundred and fifty or two hundred acres of land, exclusive of populous towns, comprehend a hundred people. It is not a small quantity of food that will suffice for so many. Ten or fifteen years' diligence, I grant, might enable Canada to perform what is now expected from her; but, in the meantime, the West Indians might have the satisfaction of starving.

To suppose the best; which is, that by applying their cane-lands to the purpose of procuring sustenance, they may preserve themselves from starving; still, the consequences must be very serious or pernicious. The wealthy planters would but ill relish the loss of their crops; and such of them as were considerably in debt would be ruined. At any rate, the revenues of Great Britain would suffer a vast diminution.

The Farmer, I am inclined to hope, builds too much upon the present disunion of Canada, Georgia, the Floridas, the Mississippi, and Nova Scotia from other colonies. A little time, I trust, will awaken them from their slumbers, and bring them to a proper sense of their indiscretion. I please myself with the flattering prospect, that they will, erelong, unite in one indissoluble chain with the rest of the colonies. I cannot believe they will persist in such a conduct as must exclude them from the secure enjoyment of those heaven-descended immunities we are contending for.

There is one argument I have frequently heard urged, which it may be of some use to invalidate. It is this: that if the mother country should be inclined to an accommodation of our disputes, we have, by our rash procedure, thrown an insurmountable obstacle in her way; we have made it disgraceful to her to comply with our requisitions, because they are proposed in a hostile manner.

Our present measures, I have proved, are the only peaceable ones we could place the least confidence in. They are the least exceptionable, upon the score of irritating Great Britain, of any our circumstances would permit. The Congress have petitioned his Majesty for the redress of grievances. They have, no doubt, addressed him in the most humble, respectful, and affectionate terms; assured him of their own loyalty and fidelity, and of the loyalty and fidelity of his American subjects in general; endeavored to convince him, that we have been misrepresented and abused; and expressed an earnest desire to see an amicable termination of the unhappy differences now existing. Can a pretext be wanting, in this case, to preserve the dignity of this parent state, and yet remove the complaints of the colonies? How easy would it be to overlook our particular agreements, and grant us redress in consequence of our petitions? It is easy to perceive there would be no difficulty in this respect.

I have omitted many considerations which might be adduced, to show the impolicy of Great Britain delaying to accommodate matters, and attempting to enforce submission, by cutting off all external sources of trade. To say all the subject allows would spin out this piece to an immoderate length. I shall therefore content myself with mentioning only three things more. First, it would be extremely hurtful to the commerce of Great Britain to drive us to the necessity of laying a regular foundation for manufactories of our own, which, if once established, could not easily, if at all, be undermined or abolished. Secondly, it would be very expensive to the nation to maintain a fleet for the purpose of blocking up our ports and destroying our trade; nor could she interrupt our intercourse with foreign climes without, at the same time, retrenching her own revenues; for she must then lose the duties and customs upon the articles we are wont to export to, and import from, them. Added to this, it would not be prudent to risk the displeasure of those nations, to whom our trade is useful and beneficial. And lastly, a perseverance in ill-treatment would naturally beget such deep-rooted animosities in America as might never be eradicated, and which might operate to the prejudice of the empire to the latest period.

Thus have I clearly proved, that the plan of opposition concerted by our Congress is perfectly consonant with justice and sound policy, and will, in all human probability, secure our freedom against the assaults of our enemies.

But, after all, it may be demanded, why they have adopted a non-exportation; seeing many arguments tend to show that a non-importation, alone, would accomplish the end desired.

I answer, that the continuance of our exports is the only thing which could lessen, or retard, the efficacy of a non-importation. It is not, indeed, probable it should do that to any great degree; but it was advisable to provide against every possible obstruction. Besides this, the prospect of its taking place, and of the evils attendant upon it, will be a prevailing motive with the ministry to abandon their malignant schemes. It will also serve to convince them that we are not afraid of putting ourselves to any inconveniences sooner than be the victims of their lawless ambition.

The execution of this measure has been wisely deferred to a future time, because we have the greatest reason to think affairs will be settled without it, and because its consequences would be too fatal to be justified by any thing but absolute necessity. This necessity there will be, should not our disputes terminate before the time allotted for its commencement.

Before I conclude this part of my address, I will answer two very

singular interrogatories proposed by the FARMER. "Can we think," says
he, "to threaten, and bully, and frighten the supreme government of the
nation into a compliance with our demands? Can we expect to force
submission to our peevish and petulant humors, by exciting clamors and
riots in England?" No, gentle sir. We neither desire nor endeavor to
threaten, bully, or frighten any persons into a compliance with our demands. We have no peevish and petulant humors to be submitted to. All
we aim at is, to convince your high and mighty master, the ministry, that
we are not such asses as to let them ride us as they please. We are determined to show them that we know the value of freedom; nor shall
their rapacity extort that inestimable jewel from us, without a manly and
virtuous struggle. But for your part, sweet sir! though we cannot much
applaud your wisdom, yet we are compelled to admire your valor, which
leads you to hope you may be able to *swear*, threaten, bully, and frighten
all America into a compliance with your sinister designs. When properly
accoutred, and armed with your formidable hickory cudgel, what may
not the ministry expect from such a champion? Alas for the poor committee gentlemen! How I tremble when I reflect on the many wounds
and scars they must receive from your tremendous arm! Alas for their
supporters and abettors! a very large part, indeed, of the continent—but
what of that? They must all be soundly drubbed with that confounded
hickory cudgel; for surely you would not undertake to drub one of them,
without knowing yourself able to treat all their friends and adherents in
the same manner, since 't is plain you would bring them all upon your
back.

I am now to address myself in particular to the Farmers of New York.

MY GOOD COUNTRYMEN:

The reason I address myself to you, in particular, is not because I am
one of your number, or connected with you in interest, more than with
any other branch of the community. I love to speak the truth, and would
scorn to prejudice you in favor of what I have to say, by taking upon me
a fictitious character, as other people have done. I can venture to assure

you the true writer of the piece signed A. W. FARMER, is not in reality a Farmer. He is some ministerial emissary, that has assumed the name to deceive you, and make you swallow the intoxicating potion he has prepared for you. But I have a better opinion of you than to think he will be able to succeed. I am persuaded you love yourselves and children better than to let any designing men cheat you out of your liberty and property, to serve their own purposes. You would be a disgrace to your ancestors, and the bitterest enemies to yourselves, and to your posterity, if you did not act like men, in protecting and defending those rights you have hitherto enjoyed.

I say, my friends, I do not address you in particular, because I have any greater connection with you than with other people. I despise all false pretensions and mean arts. Let those have recourse to dissimulation and falsehood, who can't defend their cause without it. 'T is my maxim to let the plain, naked truth speak for itself: and if men won't listen to it, 't is their own fault: they must be contented to suffer for it. I am neither merchant nor farmer. I address you, because I wish well to my country, and of course to you, who are one chief support of it; and because an attempt has been made to lead you astray in particular. You are the men, too, who would lose most, should you be foolish enough to coun-teract the prudent measures our worthy Congress has taken for the pres-ervation of our liberties. Those who advise you to do it are not your friends, but your greatest foes. They would have you made slaves, that they may pamper themselves with the fruits of your honest labor. 'T is the Farmer who is most oppressed in all countries where slavery prevails.

You have seen how clearly I have proved, that a non-importation and a non-exportation are the only peaceable means in our power to save ourselves from the most dreadful state of slavery. I have shown there is not the least hope to be placed in any thing else. I have confuted all the principal cavils raised by the pretended Farmer; and I hope, before I finish, to satisfy you, that he has attempted to frighten you with the prospect of evils which will never happen. This, indeed, I have, in a great measure, done already, by making appear the great probability, I may almost say, certainty, that our measures will procure us the most speedy redress.

Are you willing, then, to be slaves without a single struggle? Will you give up your freedom, or, which is the same thing, will you resign all security for your life and property, rather than endure some small present inconveniences? Will you not take a little trouble to transmit the advantages you now possess to those who are to come after you? I cannot doubt it. I would not suspect you of so much baseness and stupidity as to suppose the contrary.

Pray, who can tell me why a farmer in America is not as honest and good a man as a farmer in England? or why has not the one as good a right to what he has earned by his labor as the other? I can't, for my life, see any distinction between them. And yet, it seems, the English farmers are to be governed and taxed by their own Assembly, or Parliament; and the American farmers are not. The former are to choose their own representatives from among themselves, whose interest is connected with theirs, and over whom they have proper control. The latter are to be loaded with taxes by men three thousand miles off; by men who have no interest or connections among them, but whose interest it will be to burden them as much as possible, and over whom they cannot have the least restraint. How do you like this doctrine, my friends? Are you ready to own the English farmers for your masters? Are you willing to acknowledge their right to take your property from you, and when they please? I know you scorn the thought. You had rather die than submit to it.

But some people try to make you believe we are disputing about the foolish trifle of three pence duty upon tea. They may as well tell you that black is white. Surely you can judge for yourselves. Is a dispute, whether the Parliament of Great Britain shall make what laws and impose what taxes they please upon us, or not; I say, is this a dispute about three pence duty upon tea? The man that affirms it deserves to be laughed at.

It is true, we are denying to pay the duty upon tea; but it is not for the value of the thing itself. It is because we cannot submit to that without acknowledging the principle upon which it is founded; and that principle is, *a right to tax us in all cases whatsoever.*

You have heretofore experienced the benefit of being taxed by your own Assemblies only. Your burdens are so light that you scarcely feel them. You'd soon find the difference, if you were once to let the Parliament have the management of these matters.

How would you like to pay four shillings a year,[1] out of every pound your farms are worth, to be squandered (at least a great part of it) upon ministerial tools and court sycophants? What would you think of giving a tenth part of the yearly products of your lands to the clergy? Would you not think it very hard to pay ten shillings sterling, per annum, for every wheel of your wagons and other carriages; a shilling or two for every pane of glass in your houses; and two or three shillings for every one of your hearths? I might mention taxes upon your mares, cows, and many other things; but those I have already mentioned are sufficient. Methinks I see you stare, and hear you ask, how you could live, if you were to pay such heavy taxes. Indeed, my friends, I can't tell you. You are to look out for that, and take care you do not run yourselves in the way of danger, by following the advice of those who want to betray you. This you may depend upon: if ever you let the Parliament carry its point, you will have these and more to pay. Perhaps, before long, your tables, and chairs, and platters, and dishes, and knives, and forks, and every thing else, would be taxed. Nay, I don't know but they would find means to tax you for every child you got, and for every kiss your daughters received from their sweethearts; and, God knows, that would soon ruin you. The people of England would pull down the Parliament House, if their present heavy burdens were not transferred from them to you. Indeed, there is no reason to think the Parliament would have any inclination to spare you. The contrary is evident.

But being ruined by taxes is not the worst you have to fear. What security would you have for your lives? How can any of you be sure you

---

1. The full price of your farms every five years.

would have the free enjoyment of your religion long? Would you put your religion in the power of any set of men living? Remember civil and religious liberty always go together: if the foundation of the one be sapped, the other will fall of course.

Call to mind one of our sister colonies, Boston. Reflect upon the situation of Canada; and then tell whether you are inclined to place any confidence in the justice and humanity of the Parliament. The port of Boston is blocked up, and an army planted in the town. An act has been passed to alter its charter; to prohibit its assemblies; to license the murder of its inhabitants; and to convey them from their own country to Great Britain to be tried for their lives. What was all this for? Just because a small number of people, provoked by an open and dangerous attack upon their liberties, destroyed a parcel of tea belonging to the East India Company. It was not public, but private property they destroyed. It was not the act of the whole province, but the act of a part of the citizens. Instead of trying to discover the perpetrators, and commencing a legal prosecution against them, the Parliament of Great Britain interfered in an unprecedented manner, and inflicted a punishment upon a whole province, "untried, unheard, unconvicted of any crime." This may be justice, but it looks so much like cruelty, that a man of a humane heart would be more apt to call it by the latter than the former name.

The affair of Canada, if possible, is still worse. The English laws have been superseded by the French laws. The Romish faith is made the established religion of the land, and his Majesty is placed at the head of it. The free exercise of the Protestant faith depends upon the pleasure of the Governor and Council. The subject is divested of the right of trial by jury, and an innocent man may be imprisoned his whole life, without being able to obtain any trial at all. The Parliament was not contented with introducing arbitrary power and Popery in Canada, with its former limits; but they have annexed to it the vast tracts of land that surround all the colonies.

Does not your blood run cold, to think that an English Parliament should pass an act for the establishment of arbitrary power and Popery in such an extensive country? If they had any regard to the freedom and happiness of mankind, they would never have done it. If they had been friends to the Protestant cause, they would never have provided such a nursery for its great enemy; they would not have given such encouragement to Popery. The thought of their conduct, in this particular, shocks me. It must shock you, too, my friends. Beware of trusting yourselves to men who are capable of such an action! They may as well establish Popery in New York, and the other colonies, as they did in Canada. They had no more right to do it there than here.

Is it not better, I ask, to suffer a few present inconveniences, than to put yourselves in the way of losing every thing that is precious? Your lives, your property, your religion, are all at stake. I do my duty. I warn you of your danger. If you should still be so mad as to bring destruction upon yourselves; if you still neglect what you owe to God and man, you cannot plead ignorance in your excuse. Your consciences will reproach you for your folly; and your children's children will curse you.

You are told, the schemes of our Congress will ruin you. You are told, they have not considered your interest; but have neglected or betrayed you. It is endeavored to make you look upon some of the wisest and best men in America as rogues and rebels. What will not wicked men attempt! They will scruple nothing that may serve their purposes. In truth, my friends, it is very unlikely any of us shall suffer much; but let the worst happen, the farmers will be better off than other people.

Many of those that made up the Congress have large possessions in land, and may, therefore, be looked upon as farmers themselves. Can it be supposed they would be careless about the farmers' interest, when they could not injure that without injuring themselves? You see the absurdity of such a supposition.

The merchants, and a great part of the tradesmen, get their living by commerce. These are the people that would be hurt most by putting a stop to it. As to the farmers, "they furnish food for the merchant and mechanic; the raw materials for most manufactures are the produce of their industry." The merchants and mechanics are already dependent

upon the farmers for their food; and if the non-importation should continue any time, they would be dependent upon them for their clothes
also.

It is a false assertion that the merchants have imported more than
usual this year. That report has been raised by your enemies, to poison
your minds with evil suspicions. If our disputes be not settled within
eighteen months, the goods we have among us will be consumed; and
then the materials for making clothes must be had from you. Manufactures must be promoted with vigor; and a high price will be given for
your wool, flax, and hemp. It will be your interest to pay the greatest
care and attention to your sheep. Increase and improve the breed as much
as possible. *Kill them sparingly,* and such only as will not be of use toward
the increase and improvement of them. In a few months we shall know
what we have to trust to. If matters be not accommodated by spring,
enlarge the quantity of your flax and hemp. You will experience the benefit of it. All those articles will be very much wanted; they will bring a
great deal higher price than they used to do. And while you are supplying
the wants of the community, you will be enriching yourselves.

Should we hereafter find it necessary to stop our exports, you can apply
more of your land to raising flax and hemp, and less of it to wheat, rye,
etc. By which means, you will not have any of those latter articles to lie
upon hand. There will be consumption for as much of the former as you
can raise; and the great demand they will be in will make them very
profitable to you.

Patience, good Mr. Critic! *Kill them sparingly,* I said. What objection
have you to the phrase? You'll tell me, it is not *classical;* but I affirm it is,
and if you will condescend to look into Mr. Johnson's dictionary, you
will find I have his authority for it. Pray, then, for the future *spare* your
wit upon such occasions, otherwise the world will not be disposed to
spare its ridicule. And though the man that *spares* nobody does not deserve to be *spared* himself, yet will I *spare* you for the present, and proceed
to things of more importance.

Pardon me, my friends, for taking up your time with this digression, but I could not forbear stepping out of the way a little to show the world I am as able a critic and as good a punster as Mr. Farmer. I now return to the main point with pleasure.

It is insinuated, "that the bustle about non-importation, etc., has its rise, not from patriotism, but selfishness"; and is only made by the merchants, that they may get a high price for their goods.

By this time I flatter myself you are convinced that we are not disputing about trifles. It has been clearly proved to you, that we are contending for every thing dear in life; and that the measures adopted by the Congress, are the only ones which can save us from ruin. This is sufficient to confute that insinuation. But to confirm it, let me observe to you, that the merchants have not been the foremost to bring about a non-importation. All the members of the Congress were unanimous in it; and *many* of them were not merchants. The warmest advocates for it, everywhere, are not concerned in trade; and, as I have before remarked, the traders will be the principal sufferers, if it should continue any time.

But it is said it will not continue, because, "when the stores are like to become empty, they will have weight enough to break up the agreement." I don't think they would attempt it: but if they should, it is impossible a few mercenary men could have influence enough to make the whole body of the people give up the only plan their circumstances admit of for the preservation of their rights, and, of course, to forfeit all they have been so long striving to secure. The making of a non-importation agreement, did not depend upon the merchants; neither will the breaking of it depend upon them. The Congress have provided against the breach of the non-importation, by the non-consumption agreement. They have resolved for themselves, and us their constituents, "not to purchase, nor use, any East India tea whatsoever; nor any goods, wares, or merchandise from Great Britain or Ireland, imported after the first of December; nor molasses, etc., from the West Indies; nor wine from Madeira or the Western Islands; nor foreign indigo." If we do not purchase, nor use, these things, the merchant will have no inducement to import them.

Hence, you may perceive the reason of a non-consumption agreement.

It is to put it out of the power of dishonest men to break the non-importation. *Is this a slavish regulation?* Or is it a hardship upon us to submit to it? Surely not. Every sensible, every good man must approve of it. Whoever tries to disaffect you to it ought to meet with your contempt.

Take notice, my friends, how these men are obliged to contradict themselves. In one place you are told, "that all the bustle about non-importation, etc., has its rise, not from patriotism, but from selfishness"; or, in other words, that it is made by the merchants, to get a higher price for their goods. In another place it is said, "that all we are doing is instigated by some turbulent men, who want to establish a republican form of government among us."

The Congress is censured for appointing committees to carry their measures into execution, and directing them "to establish such further regulations as they may think proper for that purpose." Pray, did we not appoint our delegates to make regulations for us? What signified making them if they did not provide some persons to see them executed? Must a few bad men be left to do what they please, contrary to the general sense of the people, without any persons to control them, or to look into their behavior, and mark them out to the public? The man that desires to screen his knavery from the public eye will answer, Yes; but the honest man, that is determined to do nothing hurtful to his country, and who is conscious his actions will bear the light, will heartily answer, No.

The high prices of goods are held up, to make you dissatisfied with the non-importation. If the argument on this head were true, it would be much better to subject yourselves to that disadvantage for a time, than to bring upon yourselves all the mischiefs I have pointed out to you. Should you submit to the claim of the Parliament, you will not only be oppressed with the taxes upon your lands, etc., which I have already mentioned, but you will have to pay heavy taxes upon all the goods we import from Great Britain. Large duties will be laid upon them at home; and the merchants, of course, will have a greater price for them, or it would not be worth their while to carry on trade. The duty laid upon paper, glass, painters' colors, etc., was a beginning of this kind. The present duty upon tea is preparatory to the imposition of duties upon all other articles. Do you think the Parliament would make such a serious matter of three pence a pound upon tea if it intended to stop there? It is absurd to imagine it. You would soon find your mistake if you did. For fear of paying a somewhat higher price to the merchants for a year or two you would have to pay an endless list of taxes, within and without, as long as you live, and your children after you.

But I trust there is no danger that the prices of goods will rise much, if at all. The same Congress that put a stop to the importation of them, has also forbid raising the prices of them. The same committee that is to regulate the one, is also to regulate the other. All care will be taken to give no cause of dissatisfaction. Confide in the men whom you, and the rest of the continent, have chosen the guardians of our common liberties. They are men of sense and virtue. They will do nothing but what is really necessary for the security of your lives and properties.

A sad pother is made, too, about prohibiting the exportation of sheep without excepting wethers.* The poor Farmer is at a mighty loss to know how wethers can improve or increase the breed. Truly I am not such a conjurer as to be able to inform him, but, if you please, my friends, I can give you two pretty good reasons why the Congress have not excepted wethers. One is, that for some time we shall have occasion for all the wool we can raise; so that it would be imprudent to export sheep of any kind. And the other is, that if you confine yourself chiefly to killing wethers, as you ought to do, you will have none to export. The gentleman who made the objection must have known these things as well as myself; but he loves to crack a jest, and could not pass by so fair an opportunity.

He takes notice of the first of these reasons himself; but in order to weaken its force cries: "Let me ask you, brother farmers, which of you would keep a flock of sheep barely for the sake of their wool?" To this he answers: "Not one of you. If you cannot sell your sheep to advantage, at a certain age, you cannot keep them to any profit." He thinks, because

* "Wethers" refers to castrated rams or male sheep.

he calls you "brother farmers," that he can cajole you into believing what he pleases; but you are not the fools he takes you for. You know what is for your own interest better than he can tell you. And we all know that, in a little time, if our affairs be not settled, the demand for wool will be very great. You will be able to obtain such a price as will make it worth your while to bestow the greatest attention upon your sheep.

In another place this crafty writer tells you that "from the day our exports from this province are stopped, the farmers may date the commencement of their ruin." He asks: "Will the shopkeeper give you his goods? Will the weaver, shoemaker, blacksmith, carpenter, work for you without pay?" I make no doubt you are satisfied, from what I have said, that we shall never have occasion to stop our exports; but if things turn out contrary to our expectation, and it should become necessary to take that step, you will find no difficulty in getting what you want from the merchants and mechanics. They will not be able to do without you; and, consequently, they cannot refuse to supply you with what you stand in need of from them. Where will the merchants and mechanics get food and material for clothing, if not from the farmer? And if they are dependent upon you for those two grand supports of life, how can they withhold what they have from you?

I repeat it, my friends, we shall know how matters are like to be settled by the spring. If our disputes be not terminated to our satisfaction by that time, it will be your business to plant large parts of your land with flax and hemp. Those articles will be wanted for manufactures; and they will yield you a greater profit than any thing else. In the interim, take good care of your sheep.

I heartily concur with the Farmer in condemning all illicit trade. Perjury is, no doubt, a most heinous and detestable crime; and, for my part, I had rather suffer any thing, than have my wants relieved at the expense of truth and integrity. I know there are many pretended friends to liberty who will take offence at this declaration; but I speak the sentiments of my heart without reserve. I do not write for a party. I should scorn to be of any. All I say is from a disinterested regard to the public weal.

The Congress, I am persuaded, were of the same opinion. They, like honest men, have, as much as was in their power, provided against this kind of trade, by agreeing to use no East India tea whatever after the first day of March next.

I shall now consider what has been said with respect to the payment of debts, and stopping of the courts of justice. Let what will happen, it will be your own faults if you are not able to pay your debts. I have told you in what manner you may make as much out of your lands as ever: by bestowing more of your attention upon raising flax and hemp, and less upon other things. Those articles (as I have more than once observed) will be in the highest demand. There will be no doing without them; and, of course, you will be able to get a very profitable price for them. How can it be, that the farmers should be at a loss for money to pay their debts at a time when the whole community must buy, not only their food, but all the materials for their clothes, from them? You have no reason to be uneasy on that account.

As to the courts of justice, no violence can, nor will, be used, to shut them up; but, if it should be found necessary, we may enter into solemn agreement to cease from all litigations at law, except in particular cases. We may regulate lawsuits in such a manner as to prevent any mischief that might arise from them. Restrictions may be laid on, to hinder merciless creditors from taking advantage of the times to oppress and ruin their debtors; but, at the same time, not to put it in the power of the debtors *wantonly* to withhold their just dues from their creditors when they are able to pay them.* The law ruins many a good honest family. Disputes may be settled in a more friendly way. One or two virtuous neighbors may be chosen by each party to decide them. If the next Congress should think any regulations concerning the courts of justice requisite, they will make them; and proper persons will be appointed to

---

* Ironically, the shutting of courts—less than peaceably—would take place a decade later in Western Massachusetts by the Shays Rebels, to prevent tax sales after post-Revolutionary taxes were substantially increased. See David Szatmary, *Shays' Rebellion* (Amherst, Mass., 1980).

carry them into execution, and to see that no individuals deviate from them. It will be your duty to elect persons whose fidelity and zeal for your interest you can depend upon, to represent you in that Congress, which is to meet in Philadelphia in May ensuing.

The Farmer cries: "Tell me not of delegates, congresses, committees, mobs, riots, insurrections, associations;—a plague on them all! Give me the steady, uniform, unbiassed influence of the courts of justice. I have been happy under their protection; and, I trust in God, I shall be so again."

I say: "Tell me not of the British commons, lords, ministry, ministerial tools, placemen, pensioners, parasites. I scorn to let my life and property depend upon the pleasure of any of them. Give me the steady, uniform, unshaken security of constitutional freedom. Give me the right to be tried by a jury of my own neighbors, and to be taxed by my own representatives only. What will become of the law and courts of justice without this? The shadow may remain, but the substance will be gone. I would die to preserve the law upon a solid foundation; but take away liberty, and the foundation is destroyed."

The last thing I shall take notice of is the complaint of the Farmer, that the Congress will not allow you "a dish of tea to please your wives with, nor a glass of Madeira to cheer your spirits, nor a spoonful of molasses to sweeten your buttermilk with." You would have a right to complain, if the use of these things had been forbidden to you alone; but it has been equally forbidden to all sorts of people. The members of the Congress themselves are no more permitted to please their wives with a dish of tea, nor to cheer their spirits with a glass of wine, nor to sweeten their buttermilk with a spoonful of molasses, than you are. They are upon a footing with you in this respect.

By Him—but, with your leave, my friends, we'll try, if we can, to do without swearing. I say, it is enough to make a man mad to hear such ridiculous quibbles offered, instead of sound argument; but so it is—the piece I am writing against contains nothing else.

When a man grows warm he has a confounded itch for swearing. I have been going, above twenty times, to rap out an oath, By *Him that made me;* but I have checked myself with the reflection, that it is rather *unmannerly* to treat Him that made us, with so much freedom.

Thus have I examined and confuted all the cavils and objections, of any consequence, stated by this Farmer. I have only passed over such things as are of little weight, the fallacy of which will easily appear. I have shown that the Congress have neither "ignorantly misunderstood, carelessly neglected, nor basely betrayed you," but that they have devised and recommended the *only* effectual means to preserve your invaluable privileges. I have proved that their measures cannot fail of success, but will procure the most speedy relief for us. I have also proved that the farmers are the people who would suffer least, should we be obliged to carry all our measures into execution.

Will you, then, my friends, allow yourselves to be duped by this artful enemy? Will you follow his advices, disregard the authority of your Congress, and bring ruin on yourselves and your posterity? Will you act in such a manner as to deserve the hatred and resentment of all the rest of America? I am sure you will not. I should be sorry to think any of my countrymen would be so mean, so blind to their own interest, so lost to every generous and manly feeling.

The sort of men I am opposing give you fair words to persuade you to serve their own turns; but they think and speak of you, in common, in a very disrespectful manner. I have heard some of their party talk of you as the most ignorant and mean-spirited set of people in the world. They say that you have no sense of honor or generosity; that you don't care a farthing about your country, children, nor any body else but yourselves; and that you are so ignorant as not to be able to look beyond the present, so that if you can once be persuaded to believe the measures of your Congress will involve you in some little present perplexities, you will be glad to do anything to avoid them, without considering the much greater miseries that await you at a little distance off. This is the character they give of you. Bad men are apt to paint others like themselves. For my part I will never entertain such an opinion of you, unless you should verify their words, by wilfully falling into the pit they have prepared for you. I flatter myself you will convince them of their error by showing the world you are capable of judging what is right and left, and have resolution to pursue it.

All I ask is that you will judge for *yourselves*. I don't desire you to take my opinion, nor any man's opinion, as the guide of your actions. I have stated a number of plain arguments. I have supported them with several well-known facts. It is your business to draw a conclusion, and act accordingly. I caution you, again and again, to beware of the men who advise you to forsake the plain path marked out for you by the Congress. They only mean to deceive and betray you. Our representatives in General Assembly cannot take any wiser or better course to settle our differences than our representatives in the Continental Congress have taken. If you join with the rest of America in the same common measure, you will be sure to preserve your liberties inviolate, but if you separate from them, and seek for redress alone, and unseconded, you will certainly fall a prey to your enemies, and repent your folly as long as you live.

May God give you wisdom to see what is your true interest, and inspire you with becoming zeal for the cause of virtue and mankind!

THE FARMER REFUTED;

OR,

A more comprehensive and impartial View of the Disputes between Great Britain and the Colonies. Intended as a further Vindication of the Congress, in answer to a Letter from a Westchester Farmer, entitled a View of the Controversy between Great Britain and her Colonies, including a Mode of determining the present Disputes, finally and effectually, etc. By a sincere friend to America. Tituli remedia pollicentur, sed pyxides ipsae venena continent—The title promises remedies, but the box itself poisons. Printed by James Rivington, 1775.

In response to Hamilton's *Full Vindication,* the Rev. Samuel Seabury blasted back in the New York press on January 5, 1775. The "Westchester Farmer's" *A View of the Controversy between Great-Britain and her Colonies* . . . (London, 1775) mocked his adversary's facile invocations of "natural rights of mankind," declaring that "Man in the state of nature may be considered as perfectly free from all restraints of law and government; and then the weak must submit to the strong." The very nature of the word "colony" meant a dependence upon the mother country, he patiently explained; and as the colonies were parts of the British Empire, that meant they were subject to the "supreme, absolute authority" which lodged in the king, nobles, and Commons in London. Since the colonies were under the British government and shared in its protection, they were obligated "to pay a reasonable and proportionate part of the expense" of administration. Moreover, he warned, "If we should succeed in depriving Great Britain of the power of regulating our trade, the colonies will soon be at variance with each other. Their commercial interests will interfere; there will be no supreme power to interpose, and discord and animosity must ensue."

Hamilton struck back within two weeks of the first appearance of Seabury's essays in Rivington's *Gazetteer,* and his rejoinder was far more polished and more than twice the length of his maiden effort. *The Farmer Refuted,* printed by Rivington as a tract, appeared on February 23, 1775.

ADVERTISEMENT

The writer of the ensuing sheets can, with truth, say more than the generality of those who either espouse or oppose the claim of the BRITISH PARLIAMENT; which is, that *his* political opinions have been the result of mature deliberation and rational inquiry. They have not been influenced by prejudice, nor by any interested or ambitious motives. They are not the *spawn* of licentious clamors, or popular declamation; but the genuine offspring of sober reason. To those who are inclined to doubt *his* sincerity, *he* begs leave to recommend a little more *charity*. To those who are possessed of greater candor, and who yet may be disposed to ask how *he* can be sure that his opinions have not been influenced by prejudice, *he* answers, Because he remembers the time when he had strong prejudices on the side *he* now opposes. His change of sentiment (*he* firmly believes) proceeded from the superior force of the arguments in favor of the American claims.

Though *he* is convinced there are too many whose judgments are led captive by the most venal and despicable motives, yet *he* does not presume to think every man who differs from him either fool or knave. *He* is sensible there are men of parts and virtue, whose notions are entirely contrary to his. To imagine there are not wise and good men on both sides must be the effect of a weak head or a corrupt heart. *He* earnestly entreats the candid attention of the judicious and well meaning, and hopes that what he has written may be read with as much impartiality and as sincere a regard to truth as the importance of the controversy demands.

THE FARMER REFUTED

February 23, 1775.

Sɪʀ:—I resume my pen, in reply to the curious epistle you have been pleased to favor me with, and can assure you that notwithstanding I am naturally of a grave and phlegmatic disposition, it has been the source of abundant merriment to me. The spirit that breathes throughout is so rancorous, illiberal, and imperious; the argumentative part of it is so puerile and fallacious; the misrepresentation of facts so palpable and flagrant; the criticisms so illiterate, trifling, and absurd; the conceits so low, sterile, and splenetic, that I will venture to pronounce it one of the most ludicrous performances which has been exhibited to public view during all the present controversy.

You have not even imposed on me the laborious task of pursuing you through a labyrinth of subtilty. You have not had ability sufficient, however violent your efforts, to try the *depths* of *sophistry;* but have barely skimmed along its *surface.* I should almost deem the animadversions I am going to make unnecessary, were it not that without them you might exult in a fancied victory, and arrogate to yourself imaginary trophies.

But while I pass this judgment, it is not my intention to detract from your real merit. Candor obliges me to acknowledge that you possess every accomplishment of a polemical writer which may serve to dazzle and mislead superficial and vulgar minds: a peremptory, dictatorial air, a pert vivacity of expression, an inordinate passion for conceit, and a noble disdain of being fettered by the laws of truth. These, sir, are important qualifications; and these all unite in you in a very eminent degree. So that though you may never expect the plaudits of the judicious and discerning, you may console yourself with this assurance, that

"Fools and witlings 'will' ev'ry sentence raise,*
And wonder, with a foolish face of praise."

You will, no doubt, be pleased with this further concession—to wit: that there is a striking resemblance between yourself and the renowned hero of the *Dunciad.* "*Pert dulness*" seems to be the chief characteristic of your genius as well as his. I might point out a variety of circumstances in which you both agree; but I shall content myself with having given the hint, and leave it to yourself and to your *other*[1] admirers, to prosecute a comparison, which will reflect so high lustre on the object of admiration.

Having thus briefly delivered my sentiments of your performance in general, I shall proceed to a particular examination of it, so far as may be requisite toward placing it in that just point of light in which it ought to stand. I flatter myself I shall find no difficulty in obviating the objections you have produced against the *Full Vindication,* and in showing that your *View of the Controversy between Great Britain and the Colonies* is not only partial and unjust, but diametrically opposite to the first principles of civil society. In doing this I may occasionally interweave some strictures on the *Congress Canvassed.*

First, then, I observe you endeavor to bring the imputation of inconsistency upon me, for writing "a long and elaborate pamphlet to justify decisions, against whose influence none but *impotent* attempts had been made." A little attention would have unfolded the whole mystery. The reason assigned for what I did was, "lest those attempts," impotent as they were, in a general sense, "might yet have a tendency to mislead and

---

* This is a line, probably quoted from memory, from Alexander Pope's "Epistle to Dr. Arbuthnot" that reads "While wits and templars every sentence raise." Another verse twelve lines on reads "I ne'er with wits or witlings passed my days." Hamilton seems to have jumbled words from the two lines, and added "fools." See Alexander Pope, *The Rape of the Lock and Other Poems,* Christopher Miller, ed. (New York, 1970), 157.

1. If we may judge from the style and turn of thought, you were pleased to be your own admirer in the *card in reply.*

prejudice the minds of a few." To prevent this, I wrote; and if I have been instrumental in preserving a single person from the baneful effects of your insidious efforts, I shall not regret the time I have devoted to that laudable purpose. To confirm or to add one friend to his country, would afford a more refined and permanent satisfaction to me than could possibly animate the breast of the proudest ministerial minion, though elevated to the pinnacle of his wished-for preferment, and basking in the sunshine of court favor as the despicable wages of his prostitution and servility.

You tell me: "I knew, that at the bar of impartial reason and common-sense the conduct of the Congress must be condemned; but was too much interested, too deeply engaged in party views and party heats, to bear this with patience. *I* had no remedy (you say) but *artifice, sophistry, misrepresentation,* and *abuse.*" These you call "my weapons, and these I wield like an old experienced practitioner."

You ask: "Is this too heavy a charge? Can you lay your hand upon your heart, and upon your honor plead not guilty?" Yes, sir, I can do more. I can make a solemn appeal to the tribunal of Heaven for the rectitude of my intentions. I can affirm, with the most scrupulous regard to truth, that I am of opinion the conduct of the Congress will bear the most impartial scrutiny; that I am not interested more than as the felicity and prosperity of this vast continent are concerned; and that I am perfectly disengaged from party of every kind.

Here, I expect you will exclaim, with your usual vehemence and indecency: "You are now espousing the cause of a party! It is the most daring impudence and falsehood to assert the contrary!" I can by no means conceive, that an opposition to a small herd of malcontents, among whom you have thought proper to rank, and a zealous attachment to the general measures of America, can be denominated the effect of a party spirit. You, sir, and your adherents may be justly deemed a faction, because you compose a small number inimical to the common voice of your country. To determine the truth of this affirmation, it is necessary to take a comprehensive view of all the colonies.

Throughout your letter, you seem to consider me as a person who has acted, and is still acting, some part in the formation and execution of public measures. You tacitly represent me as a Delegate, or member of the Committee. Whether this be done with a design to create a suspicion of my sincerity, or whether it be really your opinion, I know not. Perhaps it is from a complex motive. But I can assure you, if you are in earnest, that you are entirely mistaken. I have taken no other part in the affair than that of defending the proceedings of the Congress, in conversation, and by the pamphlet I lately published. I approved of them, and thought an undeviating compliance with them essential to the preservation of American freedom. I shall therefore strenuously exert myself for the promotion of that valuable end.

In the field of literary contention, it is common to see the epithets *artifice, sophistry, misrepresentation,* and *abuse,* mutually bandied about. Whether they are more justly applicable to you, or to me, the public must decide. With respect to abuse, I make not the least doubt but every reader will allow you to surpass me in that.

Your envenomed pen has endeavored to sully the characters of our continental representatives with the presumptuous charges of ignorance, knavery, sedition, rebellion, treason, and tyranny—a tremendous catalogue indeed! Nor have you treated their friends and adherents with any greater degree of complaisance. You have also delineated the mercantile body as entirely devoid of principle; and the several committees, as bands of robbers and petty tyrants. In short, except the few who are of your own complexion and stamp, "the *virtuous* friends of order and good government," you have not hesitated to exercise your obloquy and malevolence against the whole continent.

These things being considered, it is manifest, that in my answer to your *Free Thoughts* I treated you with more lenity than you had a right to expect; and did by no means observe the strict law of retaliation. None but yourself will think you can, with the least propriety, complain of abuse.

I congratulate myself upon the sentiments you entertain of my last performance. Such is my opinion of your abilities as a critic, that I very much prefer your disapprobation to your applause. But with respect to the *brilliancy* of thought you speak of, give me leave to inform you, that I aimed at nothing more than justness of thought. I addressed myself to the judgment, not to the imagination. In works where fancy is predominant, as is the case with yours, there is a better opportunity for displaying brilliancy of thought than where reason presides and directs. No wonder, then, if you have excelled me in this particular, since your plan is so much more favorable to it than mine.

I shall, for the present, pass over that part of your pamphlet in which you endeavor to establish the supremacy of the British Parliament over America. After a proper *éclaircissement* of this point, I shall draw such inferences as will sap the foundation of everything you have offered.

The first thing that presents itself is a wish, that "I had, explicitly, declared to the public my ideas of the *natural rights* of mankind. Man, in a state of nature (you say), may be considered as perfectly free from all restraint of *law* and *government;* and then, the weak must submit to the strong."

I shall, henceforth, begin to make some allowance for that enmity you have discovered to the *natural rights* of mankind. For, though ignorance of them, in this enlightened age, cannot be admitted as a sufficient excuse for you, yet it ought, in some measure, to extenuate your guilt. If you will follow my advice, there still may be hopes of your reformation. Apply yourself, without delay, to the study of the law of nature. I would recommend to your perusal, Grotius, Puffendorf, Locke, Montesquieu, and Burlemaqui. I might mention other excellent writers on this subject; but if you attend diligently to these, you will not require any others.

There is so strong a similitude between your political principles and those maintained by Mr. Hobbes, that, in judging from them, a person might very easily *mistake* you for a disciple of his. His opinion was exactly coincident with yours, relative to man in a state of nature. He held, as you do, that he was then perfectly free from all restraint of *law* and *government.* Moral obligation, according to him, is derived from the introduction of civil society; and there is no virtue but what is purely artificial, the mere contrivance of politicians for the maintenance of social intercourse. But the reason he ran into this absurd and impious doctrine was, that he disbelieved the existence of an intelligent, superintending principle, who is the governor, and will be the final judge, of the universe.

As you sometimes swear *by Him that made you,* I conclude your sentiments do not correspond with his in that which is the basis of the doctrine you both agree in; and this makes it impossible to imagine whence this congruity between you arises. To grant that there is a Supreme Intelligence who rules the world and has established laws to regulate the actions of His creatures, and still to assert that man, in a state of nature, may be considered as perfectly free from all restraints of *law* and *government,* appears, to a common understanding, altogether irreconcilable.

Good and wise men, in all ages, have embraced a very dissimilar theory. They have supposed that the Deity, from the relations we stand in to Himself and to each other, has constituted an eternal and immutable law, which is indispensably obligatory upon all mankind, prior to any human institution whatever.

This is what is called the law of nature, "which, being coeval with mankind, and dictated by God himself, is, of course, superior in obligations to any other. It is binding over all the globe, in all countries, and at all times. No human laws are of any validity, if contrary to this; and such of them as are valid derive all their authority, mediately or immediately, from this original."—BLACKSTONE.*

---

* The quotation is from William Blackstone's *Commentaries on the Laws of England,* sec. II, "Of the Nature of Laws in General," 1:41. [Howsoever Blackstone defended the Law of Nature, he could not countenance revolution: "It must be owned that Mr. Locke, and other theoretical writers, have held, that 'there remains still inherent in the people a supreme power to remove or alter the legislative, when they find the legislative act contrary to the trust reposed in them: for, when such trust is abused, it is therefore forfeited, and devolves to those who gave it.' But however just this conclusion may be in theory,

Upon this law depend the natural rights of mankind: the Supreme Being gave existence to man, together with the means of preserving and beautifying that existence. He endowed him with rational faculties, by the help of which to discern and pursue such things as were consistent with his duty and interest; and invested him with an inviolable right to personal liberty and personal safety.

Hence, in a state of nature, no man had any *moral* power to deprive another of his life, limbs, property, or liberty; nor the least authority to command or exact obedience from him, except that which arose from the ties of consanguinity.

Hence, also, the origin of all civil government, justly established, must be a voluntary compact between the rulers and the ruled, and must be liable to such limitations as are necessary for the security of the *absolute rights* of the latter; for what original title can any man, or set of men, have to govern others, except their own consent? To usurp dominion over a people in their own despite, or to grasp at a more extensive power than they are willing to intrust, is to violate that law of nature which gives every man a right to his personal liberty, and can therefore confer no obligation to obedience.

"The principal aim of society is to protect individuals in the enjoyment of those absolute rights which were vested in them by the immutable laws of nature, but which could not be preserved in peace without that mutual assistance and intercourse which is gained by the institution of friendly and social communities. Hence it follows, that the first and primary end of human laws is to maintain and regulate these *absolute rights* of individuals."—BLACKSTONE.*

---

we cannot adopt it, nor argue from it, under any dispensation of government at present actually existing. No human laws will therefore suppose a case, which at once must destroy all law, and compel men to build afresh upon a new foundation; nor will they make a provision for so desperate an event, as must render all legal provisions ineffectual." Ibid., 161–62.]

* Ibid., 43.

If we examine the pretensions of Parliament by this criterion, which is evidently a good one, we shall presently detect their injustice. First, they are subversive of our natural liberty, because an authority is assumed over us which we by no means assent to. And, secondly, they divest us of that moral security for our lives and properties, which we are entitled to, and which it is the primary end of society to bestow. For such security can never exist while we have no part in making the laws that are to bind us, and while it may be the interest of our uncontrolled legislators to oppress us as much as possible.

To deny these principles will be not less absurd than to deny the plainest axioms. I shall not, therefore, attempt any further illustration of them.

You say: "When I assert that since Americans have not, by any act of theirs, empowered the British Parliament to make laws for them, it follows they can have no just authority to do it, I advance a position subversive of that dependence which all colonies must, from their very nature, have on the mother country." The premises from which I drew this conclusion are indisputable. You have not detected any fallacy in them, but endeavor to overthrow them by deducing a false and imaginary consequence. My principles admit the only dependence which can subsist, consistent with any idea of civil liberty, or with the future welfare of the British empire, as will appear hereafter.

"The dependence of the colonies on the mother country," you assert, "has ever been acknowledged. It is an impropriety of speech to talk of an independent colony. The words independent and colony convey contradictory ideas; much like *killing* and *sparing*.[2] As soon as a colony be-

---

2. I find, sir, you take a particular delight in persisting in absurdity. But if you are not totally incorrigible, the following interpretation of the unfortunate *adverb* will secure it from any future stripes. It is taken from Johnson's *Dictionary:* SPARINGLY, not abundantly, *Bacon;* 2, frugally, persimoniously; not lavishly, *Hayward;* with abstinence, *Atterbury;* cautiously, tenderly. Substitute *frugally* or *not lavishly* for *sparingly,* and you must blush at your own conceit. "Kill your sheep *frugally* or *not lavishly.*" Where is the impropriety of this?

comes independent on the parent state it ceases to be any longer a colony, just as when you *kill* a sheep you cease to *spare* him."

In what sense the dependence of the colonies on the mother country has been acknowledged, will appear from those circumstances of their political history which I shall, by and by, recite. The term colony signifies nothing more than a body of people drawn from the mother country to inhabit some distant place, or the country itself so inhabited. As to the degrees and modifications of that subordination which is due to the parent state, these must depend upon other things besides the mere act of emigration to inhabit or settle a distant country. These must be ascertained by the spirit of the constitution of the mother country, by the compacts for the purpose of colonizing, and more especially by the law of nature, and that *supreme law* of every society—*its own happiness.*

The idea of colony does not involve the idea of slavery. There is a wide difference between the dependence of a free people and the submission of slaves. The former I allow, the latter I reject with disdain. Nor does the notion of a colony imply any subordination to our fellow-subjects in the parent state while there is one common sovereign established. The dependence of the colonies on Great Britain is an ambiguous and equivocal phrase. It may either mean dependence on the people of Great Britain or on the king. In the former sense, it is absurd and unaccountable; in the latter, it is just and rational. No person will affirm that a French colony is independent on the parent state, though it acknowledge the king of France as rightful sovereign. Nor can it with any greater propriety be said that an English colony is independent while it bears allegiance to the king of Great Britain. The difference between their dependence is only that which distinguishes civil liberty from slavery, and results from the different genius of the French and English constitutions.

But you deny that "we can be liege subjects to the king of Great Britain while we disavow the authority of Parliament." You endeavor to prove it thus:[3] "The king of Great Britain was placed on the throne by virtue of

3. *Vide* "Congress Canvassed."

an Act of Parliament, and he is king of America by virtue of being king of Great Britain. He is therefore king of America by Act of Parliament; and if we disclaim that authority of Parliament which made him our king, we, in fact, reject him from being our king, for we disclaim that authority by which he is king at all."

Admitting that the king of Great Britain was enthroned by virtue of an Act of Parliament, and that he is king of America because he is king of Great Britain, yet the Act of Parliament is not the *efficient cause* of his being the king of America. It is only the *occasion* of it. He is king of America by virtue of a compact between us and the kings of Great Britain. These colonies were planted and settled by the grants, and under the protection, of English kings, who entered into covenants with us, for themselves, their heirs, and successors; and it is from these covenants that the duty of protection on their part, and the duty of allegiance on ours, arise.

So that to disclaim the authority of a British Parliament over us does by no means imply the dereliction of our allegiance to British monarchs. Our compact takes no cognizance of the manner of their accession to the throne. It is sufficient for us that they are kings of England.

The most valid reasons can be assigned for our allegiance to the king of Great Britain, but not one of the least force or plausibility for our subjection to parliamentary decrees.

We hold our lands in America by virtue of charters from British monarchs, and are under no obligations to the Lords or Commons for them. Our title is similar, and equal, to that by which they possess their lands; and the king is the legal fountain of both. This is one grand source of our obligation to allegiance.

Another, and the principal source, is that protection which we have hitherto enjoyed from the kings of Great Britain. Nothing is more common than to hear the votaries of Parliament urge the protection we have received from the mother country as an argument for submission to its claims. But they entertain erroneous conceptions of the matter. The king himself, being the supreme executive magistrate, is regarded by the constitution as the supreme protector of the empire. For this purpose he is the generalissimo, or first in military command. In him is vested the power of making war and peace, of raising armies, equipping fleets, and directing all their motions. He it is that has defended us from our enemies, and to him alone we are obliged to render allegiance and submission.

The law of nature, and the British constitution, both confine allegiance to the person of the king, and found it upon the principle of protection. We may see the subject discussed at large in the case of Calvin. The definition given of it by the learned Coke is this: "Legiance is the mutual bond and obligation between the king and his subjects; whereby subjects are called his liege subjects, because they are bound to obey and serve him; and he is called their liege lord, because he is bound to maintain and defend them."* Hence it is evident, that while we enjoy the protection of the king it is incumbent upon us to obey and serve him, without the interposition of parliamentary supremacy.

The right of Parliament to legislate for us cannot be accounted for upon any reasonable grounds. The constitution of Great Britain is very properly called a limited monarchy; the people having reserved to themselves a share in the legislature, as a check upon the regal authority, to prevent its degenerating into despotism and tyranny. The very aim and intention of the democratical part, or the House of Commons, is to secure the rights of the people. Its very being depends upon those rights. Its whole power is derived from them, and must be terminated by them.

It is the unalienable birthright of every Englishman, who can be considered as a *free agent,* to participate in framing the laws which are to bind him, either as to his life or property. But as many inconveniences would result from the exercise of this right in person, it is appointed by the constitution that he shall delegate it to another. Hence he is to give his vote in the election of some person he chooses to confide in as his representative. This right no power on earth can divest him of. It was

---

* The quotation is from Lord Coke, "Calvin's Case," Coke's 7 *King's Bench Reports,* 5.

enjoyed by his ancestors time immemorial, recognized and established by Magna Charta, and is essential to the existence of the constitution. Abolish this privilege, and the House of Commons is annihilated.

But what was the use and design of this privilege? To secure his life and property from the attacks of exorbitant power. And in what manner is this done? By giving him the election of those who are to have the disposal and regulation of them, and whose interest is in every respect connected with his.

The representative, in this case, is bound, by every possible tie, to consult the advantage of his constituents. Gratitude for the high and honorable trust reposed in him demands a return of attention and regard to the advancement of their happiness. Self-interest, that most powerful incentive of human actions, points and attracts toward the same object.

The duration of his trust is not perpetual, but must expire in a few years, and if he is desirous of the future favor of his constituents, he must not abuse the present instance of it, but must pursue the end for which he enjoys it, otherwise he forfeits it and defeats his own purpose. Besides, if he consent to any laws hurtful to his constituents, he is bound by the same, and must partake the disadvantage of them. His friends, relations, children, all whose ease and comfort are dear to him, will be in a like predicament. And should he concur in any flagrant acts of injustice or oppression, he will be within the reach of popular vengeance; and this will restrain him within due bounds.

To crown the whole, at the expiration of a few years, if their representatives have abused their trust, the people have it in their power to change them, and to elect others who may be more faithful and more attached to their interest.

These securities, the most powerful that human affairs will admit of, have the people of Britain for the good deportment of their representatives toward them. They may have proved, at some times, and on some occasions, defective; but, upon the whole, they have been found sufficient.

When we ascribe to the British House of Commons a jurisdiction over the colonies, the scene is entirely reversed. All these kinds of security immediately disappear; no ties of gratitude or interest remain. Interest, indeed, may operate to our prejudice. To oppress us may serve as a recommendation to their constituents, as well as an alleviation of their own incumbrances. The British patriots may, in time, be heard to court the gale of popular favor by boasting their exploits in laying some new impositions on their American vassals, and by that means lessening the burthens of their friends and fellow-subjects.

But what merits still more serious attention is this: there seems to be already a jealousy of our dawning splendor. It is looked upon as portentous of approaching independence. This, we have reason to believe, is one of the principal incitements to the present rigorous and unconstitutional proceedings against us. And though it may have chiefly originated in the calumnies of designing men, yet it does not entirely depend upon adventitious or partial causes, but is also founded in the circumstances of our country and situation. The boundless extent of territory we possess, the wholesome temperament of our climate, the luxuriance and fertility of our soil, the variety of our products, the rapidity of the growth of our population, the industry of our countrymen, and the commodiousness of our ports, naturally lead to a suspicion of independence, and would always have an influence pernicious to us. Jealousy is a predominant passion of human nature, and is a source of the greatest evils. Whenever it takes place between rulers and their subjects, it proves the bane of civil society.

The experience of past ages may inform us, that when the circumstances of a people render them distressed their rulers generally recur to severe, cruel, and oppressive measures. Instead of endeavoring to establish their authority in the *affection* of their subjects, they think they have no security but in their *fear*. They do not aim at gaining their fidelity and obedience by making them flourishing, prosperous, and happy, but by rendering them abject and dispirited. They think it necessary to intimidate and awe them to make every accession to their own power, and to impair the people's as much as possible.

One great engine to affect this in America would be a large standing army, maintained out of our own pockets, to be at the devotion of our oppressors. This would be introduced under pretext of defending us, but, in fact, to make our bondage and misery complete.

We might soon expect the martial law, universally prevalent to the abolition of trials by juries, the *Habeas Corpus* act, and every other bulwark of personal safety, in order to overawe the honest assertors of their country's cause. A numerous train of *court dependents* would be created and supported at our expense. The value of all our possessions, by a complication of extorsive measures, would be gradually depreciated till it became a mere shadow.

This will be called too high-wrought a picture, a phantom of my own deluded imagination. The highest eulogies will be lavished on the wisdom and justice of the British nation. But deplorable is the condition of that people who have nothing else than the wisdom and justice of another to depend upon.

"Political writers," says a celebrated author,[4] "have established it as a maxim, that, in contriving any system of government, and fixing the several checks and controls of the constitution, *every man* ought to be supposed a *knave,* and to have no other end, in all his actions, but *private interest.* By this interest we must govern him, and by means of it *make him co-operate to public good,* notwithstanding his insatiable avarice and ambition. Without this we shall in vain boast of the advantages of *any constitution,* and shall find, in the end, that we have no security for our liberties, and possessions except the *good-will* of our rulers—that is, we should have *no security at all.*

"It is therefore a just *political* maxim, that *every man must be supposed a knave.* Though, at the same time, it appears somewhat strange, that a maxim should be true in politics which is false in fact. But to satisfy us on this head, we may consider that men are generally more honest in a private than in a public capacity, and will go greater lengths to serve a

4. Hume, vol. I., essay V.

party than when their own private interest is alone concerned. Honor is a great check upon mankind. But where a considerable body of men act together, this check is in a great measure removed, since a man is sure to be approved by his own party for what promotes the common interest, and he soon learns to despise the clamors of adversaries. To this we may add, that every court or senate, is determined by the greater number of voices; so that, if self-interest influences only the majority (as it will always do), the whole senate follows the allurements of this separate interest, and acts as if it contained not one member who had any regard to public interest and liberty."* What additional force do these observations acquire when applied to the dominion of one community over another!

From what has been said, it is plain that we are without those checks upon the representatives of Great Britain which alone can make them answer the end of their appointment with respect to us—which is the preservation of the rights and the advancement of the happiness of the governed. The direct and inevitable consequence is, *they have no right to govern us.*

Let us examine it in another light. The House of Commons receives all its authority from its electors, in consequence of the right they have to a share in the legislature. Its electors are freeholders, citizens, and others, in Great Britain. It follows, therefore, that all its authority is confined to Great Britain. This is demonstrative. Sophistry, by an artful play of ambiguous terms, may perplex and obscure it, but reason can never confute it. The power which one society bestows upon any man, or body of men, can never extend beyond its own limits. The people of Great Britain may confer an authority over themselves, but they can never confer any over the people of America, because it is impossible for them to give *that* to another which they never possessed themselves. Now I should be glad to see an attempt to prove that a freeholder, citizen, or

* David Hume, "Of the Independency of Parliament," *Essays, Moral, Political, and Literary,* Eugene Miller, ed. (Indianapolis, 1985), 42–43.

any other man in Great Britain, has any inherent right to the life, property, or liberty, of a freeholder, citizen, or any other man in America. He
can have no original and intrinsic right, because nature has distributed
an equality of rights to every man. He can have no secondary or derivative
right, because the only thing which could give him that is wanting—the
consent of the natural proprietor. It is incumbent upon you to demonstrate the existence of such a right, or anything else you may produce
will be of little avail. I do not expect you will be discouraged at the
apparent difficulty. It is the peculiar province of an enterprising genius
to surmount the greatest obstacles, and you have discovered an admirable
dexterity in this way. You have put to flight some of my best arguments,
with no greater pains than a few positive assertions and as many paltry
witticisms; and you become altogether irresistible by adding, with a
proper degree of confidence, *You know the case to be as I state it.*

When I say that the authority of Parliament is confined to Great
Britain, I speak of it in its primitive and original state. Parliament may
acquire an incidental influence over others, but this must be by their own
free consent; for, without this, any power it might exercise would be mere
usurpation, and by no means a just authority.

The best way of determining disputes and of investigating truth, is by
descending to elementary principles. Any other method may only be-
wilder and misguide the understanding, but this will lead to a convincing
and satisfactory crisis. By observing this method, we shall learn the following truths:

That the existence of the House of Commons depends upon the people's right to a share in the legislature, which is exercised by means of
electing the members of that House. That the end and intention of this
right is to preserve the life, property, and liberty of the subject from the
encroachments of oppression and tyranny.

That this end is accomplished by means of the *intimate connection* of
interest between those members and their constituents, the people of
Great Britain.

That with respect to the people of America there is no such *intimate
connection* of interest, but the contrary, and therefore that end could not

be answered to them; consequently, the *end* ceasing, the *means* must cease also.

The House of Commons derives all its power from its own real constituents, who are the people of Great Britain; and that, therefore, it has no power but what they *originally* had in themselves.

That they had no original right to the life, property, or liberty of Americans, nor any acquired from their own consent, and of course could give no authority over them.

That therefore the House of Commons has no such authority.

What need is there of a multiplicity of arguments or a long chain of reasoning to inculcate these luminous principles? They speak the plainest language to every man of common-sense, and must carry conviction where the mental eye is not bedimmed by the mist of prejudice, partiality, ambition, or avarice. Let us now see what has been offered in opposition to them.

But, by the way, let me remark, that I have levelled my battery chiefly against the authority of the House of Commons over America, because if that be proved not to exist, the dispute is at an end. The efficacy of Acts of Parliament depends upon the due authority of the respective branches to bind the different orders and ranks of the nation.

It is said that "in every government there must be a supreme absolute authority lodged somewhere. In arbitrary governments, this power is in the monarch; in aristocratical governments, the nobles; in democratical, in the people, or the deputies of their electing. Our own government being a mixture of all these kinds, the supreme authority is vested in the king, nobles, and people—*i.e.,* the King, House of Lords, and House of Commons *elected by the people.* The supreme authority extends as far as the British dominions extend. To suppose a part of the British dominions which is not subject to the power of the British legislature, is no better sense than to suppose a country, at one and the same time to be, and not to be, a part of the British dominions. If, therefore, the colony of New York is a part of the British dominions, the colony of New York is subject to, and dependent on, the supreme legislative authority of Great Britain."

This argument is the most specious of any the advocates for parliamentary supremacy are able to produce; but when we come to anatomize and closely examine, every part of it, we shall discover that it is entirely composed of distorted and misapplied principles, together with ambiguous and equivocal terms.

The first branch is: That "in every government, there must be a supreme, absolute authority lodged somewhere." This position, when properly explained, is evidently just. In every civil society there must be a supreme power to which all the members of that society are subject, for otherwise there could be no supremacy or subordination—that is, no government at all. But no use can be made of this principle beyond matter of fact. To infer from thence, that unless a supreme, absolute authority be vested in one part of an empire over all the other parts there can be no government in the whole, is false and absurd. Each branch may enjoy a distinct, complete legislature, and still good government may be preserved everywhere. It is in vain to assert that two or more distinct legislatures cannot exist in the same state. If by the same state, be meant the same individual community, it is true. Thus, for instance, there cannot be two supreme legislatures in Great Britain, nor two in New York. But if by the same state be understood a number of individual societies or bodies politic united under one common head, then I maintain that there may be one distinct, complete legislature in each. Thus there may be one in Great Britain, another in Ireland, and another in New York; and still these several parts may form but one state. In order to do this there must indeed be some connecting, pervading principle; but this is found in the person and prerogative of the king. He it is that conjoins all these individual societies into one great body politic. He it is that is to preserve their mutual connection and dependence, and make them all co-operate to one common end—the general good. His power is equal to the purpose, and his interest binds him to the due prosecution of it.

Those who aver that the independency of America on the British Parliament implies two sovereign authorities in the same state, deceive themselves, or wish to deceive others, in two ways: by confounding the idea of the same state with that of the same individual society; and by losing sight of that share which the king has in the sovereignty, both of Great Britain and America. Perhaps, indeed, it may with propriety be said that the king is the only sovereign of the empire. The part which the people have in the legislature may more justly be considered as a limitation of the sovereign authority, to prevent its being exercised in an oppressive and despotic manner. Monarchy is universally allowed to predominate in the constitution. In this view, there is not the least absurdity in the supposition, that Americans have a right to a limitation similar to that of the people of Great Britain. At any rate, there can never be said to be two sovereign powers in the same state, while *one common king* is acknowledged by every member of it.

Let us, for a moment, imagine the legislature of New York independent on that of Great Britain. Where would be the mighty inconvenience? How would government be frustrated or obstructed by this means? In what manner would they interfere with each other? In none that I can perceive. The affairs of government might be conducted with the greatest harmony, and by the mediation of the king directed to the same end. He (as I before observed) will be the great connecting principle. The several parts of the empire, though otherwise independent on each other, will all be dependent on him. He must guide the vast and complicated machine of government, to the reciprocal advantage of all his dominions. There is not the least contradiction in this; no *imperium in imperio*, as is maintained: for the power of every distinct branch will be limited to itself, and the authority of his Majesty over the whole will, like a central force, attract them all to the same point.

The second part of your paragraph is this: "In arbitrary governments this (supreme absolute) power is in the monarch; in aristocratical governments, in the nobles; in democratical, in the people, or the deputies of their electing. Our own government, being a mixture of all these kinds, the supreme authority is vested in the king, nobles, and people—that is, in the King, House of Lords, and House of Commons elected by the people."

You are mistaken when you confine arbitrary government to a monarchy. It is not the supreme power being placed in one, instead of many, that discriminates an arbitrary from a free government. When any people are ruled by laws, in framing which they have no part, that are to bind them, to all intents and purposes, without, in the same manner, binding the legislators themselves, they are, in the strictest sense, slaves; and the government, with respect to them, is despotic. Great Britain is itself a free country, but it is only so because its inhabitants have a share in the legislature. If they were once divested of that they would cease to be free. So that, if its jurisdiction be extended over other countries that have no actual share in its legislature, it becomes arbitrary to them, because they are destitute of those checks and controls which constitute that *moral* security which is the very essence of civil liberty.

I will go farther and assert that the authority of the British Parliament over America would, in all probability, be a more intolerable and excessive species of despotism than an absolute monarchy.[5] The power of an absolute prince is not temporary, but perpetual. He is under no temptation to purchase the favor of one part of his dominions at the expense of another, but it is his interest to treat them all upon the same footing. Very different is the case with regard to the Parliament. The Lords and Commons, both, have a private and separate interest to pursue. They must be wonderfully disinterested, if they would not make us bear a very

---

5. Mr Hume, in enumerating these political maxims, which will be eternally true, speaks thus: "It may easily be observed, that though free governments have been commonly the most happy, for those who partake of their freedom, yet are they most ruinous and oppressive to *their provinces.*" He goes on to give many solid reasons for this; and, among other things, observes, that "a free state necessarily makes a great distinction (between herself and the provinces), and must continue to do so, till men learn to love their neighbors as well as themselves." He confirms his reflections by many historical facts, and concludes them thus: "Compare the *pais conquis* of France with Ireland, and you will be convinced of this truth; though this latter kingdom, being in a good measure peopled from England, possesses so many rights and privileges as should naturally make it challenge better treatment." [David Hume, "That Politics May Be Reduced to a Science," *Essays*, 18–19.]

disproportional part of the public burthens, to avoid them as much as possible themselves. The people of Britain must, *in reality,* be an order of superior beings, not cast in the same mould with the common degenerate race of mortals, if the sacrifice of our interest and ease to theirs be not extremely welcome and alluring. But should experience teach us that they are only mere mortals, fonder of themselves than their neighbors, the philanthropy and integrity of their representatives will be of a transcendent and matchless nature, should they not gratify the natural propensities of their constituents, in order to ingratiate themselves and enhance their popularity.

When you say that "our government being a mixture of all these kinds, the supreme authority is vested in the king, nobles, and *people*—that is, the King, House of Lords, and House of Commons *elected by the people,*" you speak unintelligibly. A person who had not read any more of your pamphlet than this passage, would have concluded you were speaking of our Governor, Council, and Assembly, whom, by a rhetorical figure, you styled "king, nobles, and people." For how could it be imagined you would call any government *our own,* with this description, that it is vested in the king, nobles, and *people,* in which *our own people* have not the *least share?* If our own government be vested in the king, nobles, and people, how comes it to pass that *our own* people have no part in it? The resolution of these questions will afford a proper field in which to display your ingenuity. You must endeavor to transmute the people of America into those of Great Britain, or your description will be considered as mere jargon by every man of sense. Perhaps you may be able, in imitation of that celebrated sophist Spinosa, to prove that they are only *modally* different, but *substantially* the same. Or, if you please, that syllogism of the schools, by which a *man* is proved a *horse,* may serve as an excellent model. If I recollect right, it is in these words:

> *Homo est* animal;
> *Equus est* animal;
> *Ergo, homo est equus,*

which is rendered thus: A man is an *animal*; A horse is an *animal*; *Therefore, a man is a horse.* By the same method of argumentation, you may prove that, as Britons and Americans are *generically* the same, they are *numerically* so, likewise, as your description implies. You may form a syllogism thus:

> Britons are men;
> Americans are the *same*;
> Therefore, Britons and Americans are the *same*.

This argument will be as good as the one I am next going to examine.

"The supreme authority," you say, "extends as far as the *British* dominions extend. To suppose a part of the *British* dominions which is not subject to the power of the British legislature, is no better sense than to suppose a country at one and the same time to be, and not to be, a part of the *British* dominions. If, therefore, the colony of New York be a part of the *British* dominions, the colony of New York is subject and dependent on the supreme legislative authority of Great Britain."

By "this supreme authority," I suppose you mean the Parliament of Great Britain. I deny that it extends as far as the *British* dominions extend, and I have given many substantial reasons for this denial, whereas you have never offered any to prove that it does. You have begged the question, and taken that for granted which is the very point in debate. As to your general position, that there must be a supreme, absolute authority lodged somewhere, I have explained in what sense it ought to be understood, and shown that the several parts of the empire may each enjoy a separate, independent legislature with regard to each other, under one common head, the king.

The seeming proof you have subjoined is entirely fallacious, and depends upon the use of the terms *British* dominions and *British* legislature in an *equivocal* sense. The former may signify countries subject either to the *king* or to the *legislature* of Great Britain. When we say French dominions, we mean countries subject to the king of France. In like manner, when we say British dominions, the most proper signification is, countries subject to the king of Great Britain. At least there is no impropriety in using it in this sense.[6]

If by the British legislature you mean nothing more than the Parliament of Great Britain, it is well; but if you affix a different idea to it, you are not *arbitrarily* to impose it upon others. If there be any *chimera* in your fond imagination which you express by that term, you must allow others to think it such. In short, if by the term you mean an authority resident in one part of his Majesty's dominions to make laws for every other part of them, you ought not to apply it in this sense till you have proved that such an authority does really exist; especially in a controversy about that very matter.

By the British dominions I mean the countries subject to his Britannic Majesty, in his royal capacity. By the British legislature I will suppose you intend simply the Parliament of Great Britain. Let us now try whether "to suppose there may be a part of his Britannic Majesty's dominions which is not subject to the Parliament be no better sense than to suppose a country, at one and the same time to be, and not to be, a part of the British dominions." It is impossible for any thing *to be* and *not to be;* but it involves no contradictions to say that a country may be in subjection to his Britannic Majesty and, in that sense, a part of the British dominions, without being at all dependent on the Parliament of Great Britain.[7] The colony of New York, therefore, may be a branch of

6. Or, if there is, all your objection accounts to this: that we have adopted an improper mode of expression; and, for the future, we may, in the language of the honorable House of Assembly, call the colonies his Majesty's American dominions.

7. I doubt not you will here be disposed to cavil, by urging that if we deny the authority of Parliament we also reject his Britannic Majesty, since he composes a part of it; but let it be considered that the Parliament, as such, is a political institution, not a *physical* being. We may deny his Majesty, in his political capacity, as a part of the legislature of Great Britain, and yet acknowledge him in a similar political capacity, as a part of the legislature of New York. This is an obvious distinction, and cannot be contested without an affront to common-sense.

the British empire, though not subordinate to the legislative authority of
Britain.

Upon the whole, if by the British dominions you mean territories
subject to the Parliament, you adhere to your usual fallacy, and suppose
what you are bound to prove. I deny that we are dependent on the legislature of Great Britain; and yet I maintain that we are a part of the
British empire—but in this sense only, as being the freeborn subjects of
his Britannic Majesty.

Thus I have fully examined that argument, which is esteemed the
bulwark of the doctrine of parliamentary supremacy, and, I flatter myself,
clearly refuted it. The main pillar being now broken down, the whole
structure may easily be demolished. I shall, therefore, proceed with alac-
rity in the completion of the work. But it is worthy of observation that
a cause must be extremely weak which admits of no better supports.

Your next argument (if it deserve the name) is this: "Legislation is not
an inherent right in the colonies; many colonies have been established
and subsisted long without it. The Roman colonies had no legislative
authority. It was not till the latter period of their republic that the privileges of Roman citizens, among which that of voting in assemblies of
the people at Rome was the principal one, were extended to the inhabitants of Italy. All the laws of the empire were enacted at Rome. Neither
their colonies nor conquered countries had any thing to do with legislation."

The fundamental source of all your errors, sophisms, and false reasonings, is a total ignorance of the natural rights of mankind. Were you once
to become acquainted with these, you could never entertain a thought,
that all men are not, by nature, entitled to a parity of privileges. You
would be convinced that natural liberty is a gift of the beneficent Creator
to the whole human race, and that civil liberty is founded in that, and
cannot be wrested from any people without the most manifest violation
of justice. *Civil liberty is only natural liberty, modified and secured by the
sanctions of civil society.* It is not a thing, in its own nature, precarious and
dependent on human will and caprice, but it is conformable to the constitution of man, as well as necessary to the *well-being* of society.

Upon this principle colonists, as well as other men, have a right to civil liberty. For if it be conducive to the happiness of society (and reason and experience testify that it is), it is evident that every society, of whatsoever kind, has an absolute and perfect right to it, which can never be withheld without cruelty and injustice. The practice[8] of Rome toward her colonies cannot afford the shadow of an argument against this. That mistress of the world was often unjust. And the treatment of her dependent provinces is one of the greatest blemishes in her history. Through the want of that civil liberty for which we are so warmly contending, they groaned under every species of wanton oppression. If we are wise we shall take warning from thence, and consider a like state of dependence as more to be dreaded than pestilence and famine.

The right of colonists, therefore, to exercise a legislative power, is an inherent right. It is founded upon the rights of all men to freedom and happiness. For civil liberty cannot possibly have any existence where the society for whom laws are made have no share in making them, and where the interest of their legislators is not inseparably interwoven with theirs. Before you asserted that the right of legislation was derived "from the indulgence or grant of the parent state," you should have proved two things: that all men have not a natural right to freedom; and that civil liberty is not advantageous to society.

"The position," you say, "that we are bound by no laws but those to which we have assented, either by ourselves or by our representatives, is a novel position, unsupported by any authoritative record of the British constitution, ancient or modern. It is republican in its very nature, and tends to the utter subversion of the English monarchy.

"This position has arisen from an artful change of terms. To say that an Englishman is not bound by any laws but those to which the representatives of the nation have given their consent, is to say what is true.

---

8. If her practice proves any thing, it equally proves that she had a right to plunder them as much as possible. This doctrine, I presume, will not be disagreeable to some ears. There are many who would rejoice to see America plundered in a like manner, provided they could be appointed the instruments.

But to say that an Englishman is bound by no laws but those to which he hath consented, in person, or by *his* representatives, is saying what never was true and never can be true. A great part of the people have no vote in the choice of representatives, and therefore are governed by laws to which they never consented, either by themselves or by *their* representatives."

The foundation of the English constitution rests upon this principle: that no laws have any validity or binding force without the consent and approbation of the *people,* given in the persons of *their* representatives, periodically elected by *themselves.* This constitutes the democratical part of the government.

It is also undeniably certain, that no Englishman who can be deemed *a free agent* in a *political* view can be bound by laws to which he has not consented, either in person or by *his* representative. Or, in other words, every Englishman (exclusive of the mercantile and trading part of the nation) who possesses a freehold to the value of forty shillings per annum has a right to share in the legislature, which he exercises by giving his vote in the election of some person he approves of as his representative.

"The true reason," says Blackstone, "of requiring any qualification with regard to property in voters, is to exclude such persons as are *in so mean a situation* that they are esteemed to have *no will* of their own. If these persons had votes, they would be tempted to dispose of them under some undue influence or other. This would give a great, an artful, or a wealthy man a larger share in elections than is consistent with general liberty. If it were probable that every man would give his vote freely and without influence of any kind, then, upon the true theory and genuine principles of liberty, every member of the community, however poor, should have a vote in electing these delegates, to whose charge is committed the disposal of his property, his liberty, and his life. But since that can hardly be expected in persons of indigent fortunes, or such as are under the immediate dominion of others, all popular states have been obliged to establish certain qualifications, whereby some who are suspected to have no will of their own are excluded from voting, in order to set other individuals, whose wills may be supposed independent, more thoroughly upon a level with each other."*

Hence, it appears that such "of the people as have no vote in the choice of representatives, and therefore are governed by laws to which they have not consented, either by themselves or by their representatives," are only those "persons who are *in so mean a situation* that they are esteemed to have *no will* of their own." Every *free agent,* every free man, possessing a freehold of forty shillings per annum, is, by the British constitution, entitled to a vote in the election of those who are invested with the disposal of his life, his liberty, and property.

It is therefore evident, to a demonstration, that unless a *free agent* in America be permitted to enjoy the same privilege, we are entirely stripped of the benefits of the constitution, and precipitated into an abyss of slavery. For we are deprived of that immunity which is the grand pillar and support of freedom. And this cannot be done without a direct violation of the constitution, which decrees to every *free agent* a share in the legislature.

It deserves to be remarked here, that those very persons in Great Britain who are *in so mean a situation* as to be excluded from a part in elections, are in more eligible circumstances than they would be in who have every necessary qualification.

They compose a part of that society to whose government they are subject. They are nourished and maintained by it, and partake in every other emolument for which they are qualified. They have, no doubt, most of them, relations and connections among those who are privileged to vote and by that means are not entirely without influence in the appointment of their rulers. They are not governed by laws made expressly and exclusively for them, but by the general laws of their country, equally obligatory on the legal electors and on the law-makers themselves. So that they have nearly the same security against oppression which the body of the people have.

* Blackstone, *Commentaries on the Laws of England,* "Of the Parliament," v. 1, ch. 2, 171.

To this we may add, that they are only under a conditional prohibition, which industry and good fortune may remove. They may, one day, accumulate a sufficient property to enable them to emerge out of their present state. Or, should they die in it, their situation is not entailed upon their posterity by a fixed and irremediable doom. They, agreeably to the ordinary vicissitudes of human affairs, may acquire what their parents were deficient in.

These considerations plainly show that the people in America, of all ranks and conditions, opulent as well as indigent (if subjected to the British Parliament), would be upon a less favorable footing than that part of the people of Great Britain who are *in so mean a situation* that they are supposed to have no will of their own. The injustice of this must be evident to every man of common-sense.

I shall now proceed to take such a survey of the political history of the colonies as may be necessary to cast a full light upon their present contest and at the same time, to give the public a just conception of the profound and comprehensive knowledge you have of the dispute, the fairness and candor with which you have represented facts, and the immaculate purity of your intentions.

But previous to this, the following observations may not be destitute of utility.

His Holiness the Pope, by virtue of being Christ's Vicegerent upon earth, piously assumed to himself a right to dispose of the territories of infidels as he thought fit. And in process of time all Christian princes learned to imitate his example, very liberally giving and granting away the dominions and property of Pagan countries. They did not seem to be satisfied with the title which Christianity gave them to the next world only, but chose to infer from thence an exclusive right to this world also.

I must refer it to sounder casuists than I am to determine concerning the consistency or justice of this principle. It is sufficient for my purpose to observe that it is the only foundation upon which Queen Elizabeth and her successors undertook to dispose of the lands in America. Whatever right, therefore, we may suppose to have existed, it was vested entirely in the crown; the nation had no concern in it. It is an invariable maxim, that every acquisition of foreign territory is at the absolute disposal of the king; and unless he annex it to the realm, it is no part of it; and if it be once alienated, it can never be united to it without the concurrence of the proprietors.

Were there any room to doubt that the sole right of the territories in America was vested in the crown, a convincing argument might be drawn from the principle of English *tenure*. By means of the *feudal* system the king became, and still continues to be, in a legal sense, the original proprietor, or lord paramount, of all the lands in England.[9] Agreeably to this rule, he must have been the original proprietor of all the lands in America, and was therefore authorized to dispose of them in what manner he thought proper.

The great inquiry, therefore, is concerning the terms on which these lands were really dispensed.

"The first charter granted by the crown for the purpose of colonization, is" not "that of King James the First to the two Virginia companies," as you assert. Previous to that there was one from Queen Elizabeth to Sir Walter Raleigh, for all the territory he might discover and plant between the thirty-third and fortieth degrees of north latitude which was not actually possessed by any Christian prince or inhabited by any Christian people; to have, hold, occupy, and enjoy the same, to him, his heirs and assigns for ever, with all *prerogatives, jurisdictions, royalties, privileges, franchises,* thereunto belonging, by sea or land; only reserving to herself, her heirs and successors, the fifth part of all gold and silver *ore* that might be acquired in those regions.

By this grant, Queen Elizabeth relinquished the whole legislative and executive power to Sir Walter, upon no other condition than simple homage, and the above-mentioned fifth part of gold and silver ore; which shows that the crown considered itself as invested with the absolute and

9. See Blackstone, vol. I.

entire disposal of the territories in America, and the passive conduct of
the nation declares its acquiescence in the same.

After many successless efforts to plant a colony in Virginia, this charter
was forfeited and abrogated by the attainder of Sir Walter Raleigh; and
then succeeded that of King James the First to the two Virginia companies, dated the 10th of April, 1606. This was afterward altered and
improved by a second charter, issued in 1609. There was also a third,
dated March 12, 1611–12. The mention of this last would not have answered your purpose, and therefore you chose to pass it over in silence.

In neither of these three is there the least reservation made of any
authority to Parliament. The colonies are considered in them as entirely
without the realm, and, consequently, without the jurisdiction of its legislature.

In the first charter from King James there are the following clauses:

"We do ordain, establish, and decree, etc., that each of the said colonies
shall have a council, which shall govern and order all matters and all
causes which shall arise, grow, or happen to or within the same, according
to such *laws, ordinances* and *instructions,* as shall be, in that behalf, given
and signed with our hand, or sign manual, and pass under the privy seal
of our realm of England.

"And that, also, there shall be a council established here in England,
which shall consist of thirteen persons, to be for that purpose appointed;
which shall have the superior managing and directing *only* of, and for,
all matters, that shall or may concern the government of the said several
colonies."

"Also, we do for us, our heirs, etc., declare, that all and every the
persons, being our subjects, which shall dwell and inhabit within every,
or any, the said several colonies, and every of their children which shall
happen to be born within any of the said several colonies, shall have and
enjoy all *liberties, franchises,* and *immunities* within any of our *other* dominions, to all intents and purposes, *as if they had been abiding and born
within our realm of England.*"*

---

* The charter granted by James, together with all the other colonial charters Hamilton

This latter declaration (to which there is one correspondent, or similar, in every American grant) plainly indicates that it was not the royal intention to comprise the colonies within the realm of England. The powers committed to the two councils demonstrate the same, for they would be incompatible with the idea of any other than distinct states.

The king could neither exercise, himself, nor empower others to exercise, such an authority as was really vested in the council, without a breach of the constitution, if the colonies had been a part of the realm, or within the jurisdiction of Parliament. Such an exertion of power would have been unconstitutional and illegal, and of course inadmissible, but we find it was never called in question by the legislature, and we may conclude from thence that America was universally considered as being without the jurisdiction of Parliament.

The second charter explains and amplifies the privileges of the company, erecting them into "one body or commonalty perpetual," and confirming to them the property of their former territories, with the addition of all the islands lying within one hundred miles of the shores of both seas; together with all "*commodities, jurisdictions, royalties, privileges, franchises,* and *pre-eminences,*" to be held by the king, his heirs and successors, "in free and common soccage." They were only to pay one fifth part of all the gold and silver ore they might find, in lieu of all *services.*

Their government was vested in a council, first appointed by the king; which, upon every necessary occasion, was to be summoned together by the company's treasurer. But immediately after the persons appointed are named in the charter, it is declared, that "the said council and treasurer, or any of them, shall be henceforth *nominated, chosen, continued, displaced, changed, altered,* or *supplied,* as death or other several occasions shall require, *out of* the company of the said adventurers, by the *voice* of the greater part of the said company and adventurers," every member newly elected to be sworn into office by the Lord Chancellor.

---

quotes or cites, may be found in Francis Thorpe, ed., *Federal and State Constitutions, Colonial Charters, and Other Organic Laws of the United States,* 7 vols. (Washington, D.C., 1907).

This council had "full power and authority to make, ordain, and establish all manner of *orders, laws, directions, instructions, forms,* and *ceremonies* of government and magistracy fit and necessary for and concerning the government of the said colony; and the same to abrogate, revoke, or change, at all times, not only within the precincts of the said colony, but also on the seas, in going or coming to or from said colony."

This charter is also silent with respect to Parliament, the authority of which is evidently precluded by the whole tenor of it.

You, sir, took no notice of the circumstance that the council was to be *nominated, chosen, continued, etc., out of* the Virginia company itself, agreeably to the voice of the majority. You omitted this, and gave quite a different turn to the matter; but herein you acted not at all discordant with your usual practice. Nor did you esteem it politic to transcribe the following clause: "that the said company, and every of them, their factors and assigns, shall be free of all subsidies and customs in Virginia, for the space of one and twenty years, *and from all taxes and impositions forever,* upon any goods or merchandises, at any time or times hereafter, either upon importation thither or exportation from thence."

The third charter is a still farther enlargement of their territory and privileges, and is that by which their present form of government is modelled. The following extract will show the nature of it: "We do hereby ordain and grant, that the said treasurer and company of adventurers and planters aforesaid shall and may, once every week, and oftener, at their pleasure, hold and keep a court or assembly, for the better order and government of the said plantation; and that any five persons of our council for the time being, of which company the treasurer, or his deputy, to be always one, and the number of fifteen persons, at the least, of the generality of the said company assembled together in such a manner as hath been heretofore used and accustomed, shall be reputed to be, and shall be, a sufficient court for the handling, ordering, and dispatching of all such casual and particular occurrences, as shall, from time to time, happen, touching and concerning the said plantation. And, nevertheless, for the handling, ordering, and disposing of the matters and affairs of greater weight and importance, such as shall, *in any sort,* concern the public weal and the general good of the said plantation, as, namely, the *manner of government,* from time to time, to be used, the ordering and disposing of the lands and possessions, and the *settling and establishing of a trade there,* or such like, there shall be held and kept, every year *for ever,* one great general and solemn assembly. In all and every of which said great and general courts, so assembled, our will and pleasure is, and we do, for us, our heirs and successors for ever, give and grant to the said treasurer and company, or the greater number of them, so assembled, that they shall and may have full power and authority, from time to time, and at all times hereafter, to *elect* and *choose* discreet persons to be of our said council, for the first colony of Virginia; and to nominate and appoint such officers as they shall think fit and requisite for the government, managing, ordering, and dispatching of the affairs of the said company; and shall likewise have full power and authority to ordain and make such laws and ordinances for the good and welfare of the said plantation as to them, from time to time, shall be thought requisite and meet; *so always, as the same be not contrary to the laws and statutes of this our realm of England.*"

By this charter, King James divested himself wholly both of the legislative and executive authority, but, for his own security, prescribed a model for their civil constitution. Their laws were not to be *contrary* to the laws and statutes of his realm of England; which restriction was inserted into all the subsequent charters, with some little variation, such as, that their laws should be "consonant to reason, and not repugnant, or contrary, but, *as near as conveniently may be,* agreeable to the laws, statutes, and rights of this our kingdom of England."

This mode of expression, so indefinite in itself, shows that the use made of the clause by some ministerial advocates, is by no means natural or warrantable. It could only be intended to set forth the British constitution as a pattern for theirs; and accordingly we find, that upon the arrival of Sir George Yardly in Virginia, soon after this patent was procured, the government was regulated upon a new plan, that it might "resemble the British constitution, composed of two Houses of Parliament and a sovereign. The number of the council was increased, intending this body should represent the House of Lords, while the House of Commons was composed of burgesses, assembled from every plantation and settlement in the country."

There might be a great dissimilarity between the laws of Virginia and those of Great Britain, and yet not an absolute contrariety; so that the clause in question is not explicit or determinate enough to authorize the conclusion drawn from it. Besides, if the colonies were within the realm of England there would be no necessity for any provision in favor of its laws; and if they were without (as is clearly implied by the clause itself), it must be a contradiction to suppose its jurisdiction could extend beyond its own limits.

But the true interpretation may be ascertained, beyond a doubt, by the conduct of those very princes who granted the charters. They were certainly the best judges of their own intention, and they have left us indubitable marks of it.

In April, 1621, about nine years after the third Virginia charter was issued, a bill was introduced into the House of Commons, for indulging the subjects of England with the privilege of fishing upon the coast of America; but the House was informed by the Secretary of State, by order of his Majesty King James, that *America was not annexed to the realm, and that it was not fitting that Parliament should make laws for those countries.*

In the reign of his successor, Charles the First (who granted the Massachusetts and Maryland charters), the same bill was again proposed in the House, and was, in the like manner, refused the royal assent, with a similar declaration that "it was unnecessary, that the colonies *were without the realm and jurisdiction of Parliament*"; circumstances which evidently prove that these clauses were not inserted to render the colonies dependent on the Parliament, but only (as I have observed) to mark out a model of government for them. If, then, the colonies were, at first, *without the realm and jurisdiction of Parliament,* no human authority could afterward alter the case, without their own voluntary, full, and express approbation.

The settlement of New England was the next in succession, and was instigated by a detestation of civil and ecclesiastical tyranny. The principal design of the enterprise was to be emancipated from their sufferings, under the authority of Parliament and the laws of England. For this purpose, the Puritans had before retired to foreign countries, particularly to Holland. But Sir Robert Naughton, Secretary of State, having remonstrated to his Majesty concerning the impolicy and absurdity of dispeopling his own dominions by means of religious oppression, obtained permission for the Puritans to take up their abode in America, where they found an asylum from their former misfortunes.

Previous to their embarkation at Holland, they had stipulated with the Virginia Company[10] for a tract of land in *contiguity* with Hudson's River; but when they arrived in America (by some misconduct of the pilot), they found themselves at Cape Cod, which was without the boundaries of the Virginia patent. There the season compelled them to remain, and there they have prosecuted their settlements.

They looked upon themselves as having reverted to a state of nature, but being willing still to enjoy the protection of their former sovereign, they executed the following instrument:

"In the name of God, Amen! We, whose names are underwritten, the loyal subjects of our dread Sovereign Lord, King James, of Great Britain, etc., *King*,[11] Defender of the Faith, etc., having undertaken for the glory of God, and the advancement of the Christian faith, and the honor of our *King* and country, a voyage to plant the first colony in the northern part of Virginia, do, by these presents, mutually, in the presence of God

10. This was after they had received their third charter.

11. This ought to silence the infamous calumnies of those who represent the first settlers in New England as enemies to kingly government, and who are, in their own opinions, wondrous witty, by retailing the idle and malicious stories that have been propagated concerning them; such as their having erased *King, Kingdom,* and the like, out of their Bibles, and inserted in their stead, Civil Magistrate, Parliament, and Republic.

and one another, covenant and combine ourselves together into a civil body politic, for our better order and preservation, and furtherance of the ends aforesaid; and by virtue hereof to enact, constitute, and frame, such just and equal laws, ordinances, acts, constitutions, and officers, from time to time, as shall be thought most meet and convenient for the general good of the colony; unto which we promise all due submission and obedience.

"In witness whereof we have hereunto subscribed our names, at Cape Cod, November 11, 1620."

This was the original constitution of New Plymouth. It deserves to be remarked here, that these first settlers possessed their lands by the most equitable and independent title, that of a fair and honest purchase from their natural owners, the Indian tribes. King James soon after erected a council at Plymouth, in the county of Devon, "for the planting, ruling, ordering, and governing of New England in America"; and granted to "them, their successors and assigns, all that part of America, lying, and being in breadth, from forty degrees of north latitude from the equinoctial line, to the forty-eighth degree of the said northerly latitude, inclusively, and in length of, and within all the breadth aforesaid, throughout all the main land, from sea to sea, together with all the firm lands, soils, grounds, havens, ports, rivers, waters, fishings, minerals, precious stones, quarries, and all and singular other commodities, *jurisdictions, royalties, privileges, franchises, and pre-eminences,* both within the said tract of land upon the main, and also within the islands and seas adjacent,—to be held of his Majesty, his heirs and successors, in free and common soccage; and the only consideration to be the fifth part of all gold and silver ore, for and in respect *of all and all manner of duties, demands, and services.*"

This council was vested with the sole power of legislation; the election and appointment of all officers, civil and military; authority to coin money, make war and peace, and a variety of other signal privileges. The colony of New Plymouth was comprehended within the grant. In consequence of which, its inhabitants, a few years after, purchased the claim of the patentees, with all their rights and immunities, and became an independent state by charter.

The same motives that induced the settlement of New Plymouth did also produce that of Massachusetts. It was first colonized by virtue of a patent from the council at Plymouth, and in a year after by a charter from King Charles the First dated the 4th of March, in the fourth year of his reign; by which the adventurers and inhabitants were formed into "one body politic and corporate, by the name of the Governor and Company of the Massachusetts Bay, in New England," and clothed with powers and privileges resembling those of the colony of New Plymouth.

It happened some time before this, that there was a dissolution of the Virginia Company by a royal proclamation dated 15th of July, 1624, by which the colony became more immediately dependent on the king. The Virginians were greatly alarmed at this, and forthwith presented a remonstrance to the Throne; in which they signified an apprehension of "designs formed against their rights and privileges." In order to banish their fears, the Lords of the Council (in a letter dated the 22d of July, 1634) gave them an assurance, by his Majesty's direction, "that all their *estates, trade, freedom,* and *privileges,* should be enjoyed by them in as extensive a manner as they enjoyed them before the recall of the company's patent." Agreeably to this, their former constitution was confirmed and continued.

The Maryland charter is the next in order, of which you, sir, have made no mention. It was granted by King Charles the First to Lord Baltimore, and contains such ample and exalted privileges, that no man in his senses can read it without being convinced it is repugnant to every idea of dependence on Parliament.

It bestows on him "all the country of Maryland, and the islands adjacent, together with all their commodities, *jurisdictions, privileges, prerogatives, royal rights,* etc., etc., of what kinds soever, as well by sea as land; and constitutes him, his heirs and assigns, true and absolute lords and proprietaries of the said country, and of all the premises aforesaid, saving always the faith and allegiance and the sovereign dominion, due to *himself,* his heirs and successors,—to be holden of the Kings of England, in free and common soccage, by *fealty only,* and not *in capite;* paying two Indian arrows every year, and also the fifth part of all gold and silver ore which shall from time to time happen to be found: Granting also full and absolute power to the said Lord Baltimore, his heirs, etc., to ordain, make, enact, and publish *any laws whatsoever, by* and *with* the *advice, assent,* and *approbation* of the *freemen* of the said province, or the greater part of them, or of *their delegates* or *deputies, whom,* for the enacting of the said laws, when, and as often as need shall require, we will, that the said now Lord Baltimore, and his heirs, shall assemble in such sort and form as to him and *them* shall seem best. Provided, nevertheless, that the said laws be consonant to reason, and be not repugnant, or contrary, but, *as near as conveniently may be,* agreeable to the laws, statutes, and rights of this our kingdom of England."

In another place it is ordained that he, the "said Lord Baltimore, *may, from time to time for ever,* have and enjoy the customs and subsidies within the said ports, harbors, etc., within the province aforesaid, payable or due for *merchandises* and *wares* there to be laden and unladen; the said *subsidies* and *customs* to be reasonably assessed (upon any occasion) by *themselves* and the *people there,* as aforesaid, to whom we give power by these presents, for us, our heirs and successors, upon just cause and in due proportion, to assess and impose the same."

I confine myself to these extracts to avoid prolixity, and pass over the enumeration of those many extensive prerogatives this charter confers: such as the appointment of all officers, civil and military; the power of making war and peace; the establishment of *boroughs* and *cities;* with all necessary immunities, and the like.

In the fourteenth year of Charles the Second, the two colonies, Connecticut and New Haven, petitioned the king to unite them into one colony, which was complied with. Privileges, as valuable and extensive as any that had been before granted, were comprised in their charter. There was only a reservation of allegiance to the king, without the smallest share of the legislative or executive power. The next year, Providence and Rhode Island procured a charter, with privileges exactly correspondent to those of Connecticut.

You are pleased to assert, "that the charters of Rhode Island and Connecticut are simply matters of incorporation"; and produce an extract in confirmation of this assertion.

I should be astonished at so extraordinary a deviation from truth, if there were not many instances similar to it. Not only the whole tenor of their charters, but their constant practice and form of government hitherto, declare the reverse of your assertion. But, that I may not unnecessarily prolong this letter by a quotation of the different parts of the respective charters, give me leave to present you with an account of the constitution of these colonies, which was laid before the House of Lords in January, 1734.

"Connecticut and Rhode Island," say the Commissioners of Trade and Plantations, "are charter governments, where almost the whole power of the crown is delegated to the people, who make annual election of their Assembly, their Councils, and their Governors; likewise to the majority of which Assemblies, Councils, and Governors, respectively, being collective bodies, the power of making laws is granted; and, as their charters are worded, they can, and do, make laws, even without the Governor's assent, no negative voice being reserved to them, as Governors, in said charters. These colonies have the power of making laws for their better government and support; and are not under any obligation, by their respective constitutions, to return authentic copies of their laws to the crown, for approbation or disallowance; nor to give any account of their proceedings; nor are their laws repealable by the crown; but the validity of them depends upon their not being contrary, but, *as nearly as may be,* agreeable to the laws of England."

As to the expression, as *other* our liege people of this our realm of England, or any *other* corporation or body politic within the same, if any stress be laid on the particle *other,* it will imply not only that the colonies were simple matters of corporation, but that the inhabitants of them were considered as being within the realm of England. But this cannot be admitted as true without contradicting other clauses of the same charters. Thus, in the preamble to that of Rhode Island, it is said that the first planters "did, by the consent of our royal progenitors, transport themselves *out* of this kingdom of England *into* America." And in each of the charters the king stipulates that all the children born in America shall enjoy "all the liberties and immunities of free and natural subjects, within any of his dominions, as *if* they and every of them *were* born within the realm of England."

The vague and improper manner in which this particle is used in many other places of the several charters will not allow it the least weight in the present instance. In the eleventh article of the third Virginia charter there is this expression: "All such, and so many of our loving subjects, or any *other* strangers that will," etc. The same rule of inference that makes Rhode Island and Connecticut simple corporations, will also transform the king's loving subjects into mere strangers, which I apprehend cannot be done without some degree of absurdity.

In the fifteenth year of Charles the Second, Carolina was erected into a principality. A patent dated March 24, 1663, was granted to eight lord proprietors, vesting them with all its rights, privileges, prerogatives, royalties, etc., and the whole legislative and executive authority, together with the power of creating a nobility. The form of government was determined by a compact between the people and the proprietors, which contained one hundred and twenty articles; and "these were to be and remain the sacred and unalterable rule and form of government in Carolina for ever." A Palatine* was to be erected from among the proprietaries, who was to govern the principality during his life; and at his demise, the surviving lords were to succeed him according to the order of seniority. The legislative power was to reside in the Parliament of that country, consisting of the Palatine as sovereign; an upper House, in which the proprietors or their deputies, the governor and the nobility, were to sit; and a lower House, *composed of the delegates of the people.* There was likewise a court established, the members of which were three proprietaries, and the Palatine as president, and in this court the whole executive authority was lodged.

---

* A Palatine refers in this context to an elective royal official; elective viceroy.

There were also several other courts: the Chief Justice's, the High Constable's, the Chancellor's, and the High Steward's Court. The principal officers of the State, in number, titles, and power, resembled those of the realm of England. The proprietors of Carolina considered themselves as possessed of every requisite toward forming a separate independent state, and were always extremely jealous of any encroachments. They even disputed the king's authority to establish Courts of Vice-Admiralty within their precincts, though for the examination and punishment of offences committed without them, and always appointed an admiral of their own. One of their governors was deposed for "accepting a commission under King William, as Judge of the Admiralty, when he had, at the same time, a commission from the Lords proprietaries for the same office."

The Philadelphia charter was next granted, and contained almost an equality of privileges with that of Maryland. There was, indeed, a reverse in favor of Parliament, perfectly singular and unprecedented in any foregoing charter, and which must either be rejected, or the general tenor of the grant becomes unintelligible.

It happened that the charter of Massachusetts was vacated by a decision in Chancery, and a new one was conferred by *William and Mary*. The agents for that colony did not accept it till they had first consulted the most judicious civilians and politicians upon the contents of it, and then drew up an instrument in which they assigned the reasons of their acceptance. The following extract will serve to show their sense of it: "The colony," say they, "is now made a province; and the General Court has, with the King's approbation, as much power in New England as the King and Parliament have in England. They have all English privileges and liberties, and can be touched by *no law* and by *no tax*, but of their own making. All the liberties of their religion are for ever secured."

You say, that "the power to levy taxes is restrained to provincial and local purposes only, and to be exercised over such only as are inhabitants and proprietors of the said province."

They are empowered "to levy proportionable and reasonable assess-

ments, rates, and taxes, for our service in the necessary defence and support of the government of the said province or territory, and the protection and preservation of the inhabitants there." The defence and support
of government, and their own protection and preservation, are the purposes for which they are to raise supplies; and, in my humble opinion,
there are no others to which any society is under an obligation to contribute its wealth or property.

I shall only make one more observation upon this charter—which is,
that there was a reservation in it of liberty for the people of England to
fish upon their coasts, which would have been useless and absurd, had
that province been a part of the realm, and within the jurisdiction of
Parliament.

Were it necessary to elucidate still more a point which is so conspicuous from the several charters of the colonies, as well as the express
declarations of those princes by whom they were granted, to wit: "*that
the colonies are without the realm and jurisdiction of Parliament,*" I might
enumerate many striking circumstances besides those I have already mentioned. But as the case is by this time sufficiently clear, I shall confine
myself to the recital of only one or two more transactions.

An act of the twenty-fifth of Charles the Second was the first that
ever imposed duties on the colonies for any purpose; and these, as the
preamble itself recites, were simply as a regulation of trade, and were of
a prohibitory nature. Notwithstanding this, it was the source of great
dissatisfaction; and was one of the principal causes of the insurrection in
Virginia, under Colonel Bacon, which after his death subsided; and then
the province sent agents to England, to remonstrate "against taxes and
impositions being laid on the colony by any authority but that of the
General Assembly." In consequence of this, a declaration was obtained,
under the privy seal of King Charles, dated nineteenth of April, 1676, to
this effect: that "taxes ought not to be laid upon the proprietors and
inhabitants of the colony, but by the common consent of the General
Assembly."

About three years after, when King Charles had occasion to raise a permanent revenue for the support of Virginia, he did not attempt to do it by means of a parliamentary donation, but framed a bill, and sent it there by Lord Culpepper, who was at that time governor, to receive the concurrence of their legislature. It was *there* passed into a law, and "*enacted by the King's most excellent Majesty, by and with the consent of the General Assembly of the colony of Virginia.*" If the Virginians had been subjects of the realm, this could not have been done without a direct violation of *Magna Charta*, which provides that no English subject shall be taxed without the consent of Parliament.

Thus, sir, I have taken a pretty general survey of the American charters, and proved, to the satisfaction of every unbiassed person, that they are entirely discordant with that sovereignty of Parliament for which you are an advocate. The disingenuity of your extracts (to give it no harsher name) merits the severest censure, and will, no doubt, serve to discredit all your former, as well as future, labors in your favorite cause of despotism.

It is true, that New York has no charter. But if it could support its claim to liberty in no other way, it might, with justice, plead the common principles of colonization: for it would be unreasonable to exclude one colony from the enjoyment of the most important privileges of the rest. There is no need, however, of this plea. THE SACRED RIGHTS OF MANKIND ARE NOT TO BE RUMMAGED FOR AMONG OLD PARCHMENTS OR MUSTY RECORDS. THEY ARE WRITTEN, AS WITH A SUNBEAM, IN THE WHOLE VOLUME OF HUMAN NATURE, BY THE HAND OF THE DIVINITY ITSELF, AND CAN NEVER BE ERASED OR OBSCURED BY MORTAL POWER.

The nations of Turkey, Russia, France, Spain, and all other despotic kingdoms in the world, have an inherent right, whenever they please, to shake off the yoke of servitude (though sanctioned by the immemorial usage of their ancestors), and to model their government upon the principles of civil liberty.

I will now venture to assert, that I have demonstrated, from the voice of nature, the *spirit* of the British constitution, and the charters of the colonies in general, the absolute non-existence of that parliamentary supremacy for which you contend. I am not apt to be dogmatical, or too confident of my own opinions; but if I thought it possible for me to be mistaken, when I maintain that the Parliament of Great Britain has no sovereign authority over America, I should distrust every principle of my understanding, reject every distinction between truth and falsehood, and fall into a universal skepticism.

Hitherto, I have reasoned against the whole authority of Parliament, without even excepting the right we have conceded, of regulating trade. I considered it, in its original state, as founded in the British constitution, the natural rights of society, and the several charters of the colonies. The power of regulating our trade was first exercised in the reign of Charles the Second. I shall not examine upon what principle. It is enough, we have consented to it. But I shall proceed to consider the argument you make use of to establish the propriety of allowing special duties to be imposed by way of tribute for the protection of our commerce.

You argue thus: "Notwithstanding the large landed estates possessed by the British subjects in the different parts of the world, they must be considered as a commercial manufacturing people. The welfare, perhaps the existence, of Great Britain as an independent or sovereign state depends upon her manufactures and trade; and many people in America think that her manufactures and commerce depend in a great measure on her intercourse with her colonies; insomuch that if this should be neglected her commerce would decline and die away, her wealth would cease, and her maritime power be at an end. If these observations be just, they establish the right of the British Parliament to regulate the commerce of the whole empire, beyond possibility of contradiction; a denial of it would be a denial of a right in the British empire to preserve itself. They prove also that all parts of the empire must be subject to the British Parliament, for otherwise the trade of the whole cannot be regulated. They point out also the best mode of raising such a revenue as is necessary for the support and defence of the government, viz.: by duties on imports and exports, because these are attended with the least inconvenience to the subject, and may be so managed as to raise a revenue and regulate the trade at the same time.

"When it is considered that Great Britain is a maritime power, that the present flourishing state of her trade and of the trade of her colonies depends in a great measure upon the protection which they receive from the navy, that her own security depends upon her navy, and that it is principally a naval protection we receive from her, there will appear a peculiar propriety in laying the chief burthen of supporting her navy upon her commerce, and in requesting us to bear a part of the expense, proportional to our ability, and to that protection and security which we receive from it."

The supposition that a cessation of commerce between Great Britain and the colonies would be ruinous and destructive to the former is ushered in as the principal argument for her right to regulate the commerce of the whole empire. I am willing to allow it its full weight, but I cannot conceive how you can pretend, after making such use of it, to deny it the force it ought to have, when it is urged as affording a moral certainty that our present measures will be successful. If you tacitly adopt the principle, and reason from it in one case, with what propriety can you reject it in the other? If the preservation of the British empire depends in any material degree upon the right of Parliament to regulate the trade of the colonies, what will be the consequence if the trade ceases altogether? You must either acknowledge that you have adduced a very weak and foolish argument, or that the commercial connection between Great Britain and the colonies is essential to her security and prosperity. You have either failed in proving your point, or you have furnished me with an ample confutation of all your reasoning against the probability of success, from the restrictions laid on our commerce. If our trade be necessary to the welfare of Great Britain, she must, of course, be ruined by a discontinuance of it.

But it is granted that Great Britain has a right to regulate the trade of the empire. The Congress have acknowledged it so far as concerned their constituents. You infer from thence that all parts of the empire must be subject to her. They need only be so far subject as is necessary for the end proposed, that is, the regulation of their trade. If you require any further subjection, you require *means* that are disproportionate to the *end*, which is unreasonable, and not at all allowable.

With respect to the justice of submitting to impositions on our trade for the purpose of raising a revenue to support the navy by which it is protected, I answer that the exclusive regulation of our commerce for her own advantage is a sufficient tribute to Great Britain for protecting it. By this means a vast accession of wealth is annually thrown into her coffers. It is a matter of notoriety that the balance of trade is very much against us. After ransacking Spain, Portugal, Holland, the English, French, Spanish, Dutch, and Danish plantations, for money and bills of exchange, as remittances for the commodities we take from Great Britain, we are still always greatly in arrears to her. At a moderate computation, I am well informed that the profits she derives from us every year exceed two millions and a half sterling; and when we reflect that this sum will be continually increasing as we grow more and more populous, it must be evident that there is not the least justice in raising a revenue upon us by the imposition of special duties.

The right of Great Britain to regulate our trade upon this plan, it is now acknowledged, is not an inconsiderable matter. It is as much as any free people can concede, and as much as any just people would require. We are not permitted to procure manufactures anywhere else than from Great Britain, or Ireland. Our trade is limited and prescribed, in every respect, as is most for her interest. This is a plentiful source of wealth to her, as I have heretofore shown, and shall hereafter confirm by the testimony of some British writers.

But I have found out an argument, which I imagine will go very near convincing yourself of the absurdity of what you have offered on this head. It is short, but conclusive. "*The principal profits of our trade centre in Great Britain.*"[12] How can you, my dear sir, after making this confes-

---

12. See page 19 of your own letter.

sion, entertain a single thought that it is incumbent upon us to suffer her to raise a revenue upon our trade? Are not the *principal profits* a sufficient recompense for protecting it? Surely you would not allow her the whole. This would be rather too generous. However ardent your affection to her, and however much it may be your glory to advance her imperial dignity, you ought to moderate it so far as to permit us to enjoy some little benefit from our trade. Only a small portion of the profits will satisfy us. We are willing to let her have the *principal* share, and this you acknowledge she already has. But why will you advise us to let her exhaust the small pittance we have reserved as the reward of our own industry in burthensome revenues? This might be liberality and generosity, but it would not be prudence; and let me tell you, in this selfish, rapacious world a little discretion is at worst only a *venial* sin. It will be expedient to be more cautious for the future. It is difficult to combat truth, and unless you redouble your vigilance you will (as in the present instance) be extremely apt to ensnare yourself.

I shall now briefly examine the excellent mode you have proposed for settling our disputes finally and effectually. All internal taxation is to be vested in our own Legislatures, and the right of regulating trade by duties, bounties, etc., to be left to the Parliament, together with the right of enacting all general laws for all the colonies. You imagine that we should then "have all the security for our rights, liberties, and properties, which human policy can give us."

Here we widely differ in sentiment. My opinion is that we should have no "security besides the goodwill of our rulers—that is, no security at all." Is there no difference between one system of laws and another? Are not some more favorable and beneficial to the subject, better calculated to preserve his life and personal liberty than others? It is evident they are. Suppose, instead of the present system established among us, the French laws were to be introduced for the good of all the colonies, should we have the same security for our lives which we now have? I presume we should not. I presume, also, that a revolution in our laws might and would gradually take place.

A fondness for power is implanted in most men, and it is natural to abuse it when acquired. This maxim, drawn from the experience of all ages, makes it the height of folly to intrust any set of men with power which is not under every possible control; perpetual strides are made after more as long as there is any part withheld. We ought not, therefore, to concede any greater authority to the British Parliament than is absolutely necessary. There seems to be a necessity for vesting the regulation of our trade *there*, because in time our commercial interests might otherwise interfere with hers. But with respect to making laws for us, there is not the least necessity, or even propriety, in it. Our Legislatures are confined to ourselves, and cannot interfere with Great Britain. We are best acquainted with our own circumstances, and therefore best qualified to make suitable regulations. It is of no force to object that no particular colony has power to enact general laws for all the colonies. There is no need of such general laws. Let every colony attend to its own internal police, and all will be well. How have we managed heretofore? The Parliament has made no general laws for our good, and yet our affairs have been conducted much to our ease and satisfaction. If any discord has sprung up among us, it is wholly imputable to the incursions of Great Britain. We should be peaceable and happy, if unmolested by her. We are not so destitute of wisdom as to be in want of her assistance to devise proper and salutary laws for us.

The legislative power of Parliament would at any rate be useless to us; and as utility is the prime end of all laws, that power has no reason for which it should exist. It is not even requisite for preserving the connection between Great Britain and the colonies, for that is sufficiently secured in two ways: by being united under the same king, and by the important privilege of regulating our commerce, to which we have submitted.

That it may be prejudicial to us no reasonable man can deny. We may trace the evils of it through the whole administration of justice. Judicial proceedings may be so ordered as to render our lives and properties dependent on the will and caprice of court favorites and tools. A wide field for bribery and corruption of every kind would be opened, and the most enormous exactions would take shelter under the garb of law. It is un-necessary to enter into a particular detail of the different methods in which all this might be effected; every man's own imagination will sug-gest to him a multiplicity of instances.

Rigorous, oppressive, and tyrannical laws may be thought expedient as instruments to humble our rebellious tempers, and oblige us to submit to further exactions of authority, till the claim to bind us in all cases whatsoever be fully complied with. This, no doubt, would be a work of time. The steps would be gradual, and perhaps imperceptible; but they would be sure and effectual. That thirst of power which influenced the Parliament to assert an unlimited authority over us, without the least plausible foundation for it (as I have clearly proved), will authorize us to apprehend the worst.

The power of legislating for us, and of raising a revenue upon the articles of commerce, would be a sufficient degree of slavery. It is absurd to say that Great Britain could not impose heavy burthens on our com-merce, without immediately feeling the effect herself. She may enrich herself by reducing us to the most lamentable state of penury and wretch-edness. We are already forbid to purchase the manufactures of any foreign countries. Great Britain and Ireland must furnish us with the necessaries we want. Those things we manufacture among ourselves may be disal-lowed. We should then be compelled to take the manufactures of Great Britain upon her own conditions. We could not, in that case, do without them. However excessive the duties laid upon them, we should be under an inevitable necessity to purchase them. How would Great Britain feel the effects of those impositions, but to her own advantage? If we might withdraw our custom and apply to other nations, if we might manufac-ture our own materials, those expedients would serve as a refuge to us, and would indeed be a security against any immoderate exactions. But these resources would be cut off. There would be no alternative left us. We must submit to be drained of all our wealth, for those necessaries which we are not permitted to get elsewhere.

As to our trade with foreign countries, the burthens imposed on that, however grievous, would in like manner affect Great Britain only by increasing her public treasure. Her own inhabitants would pay no part of them; they would fall solely upon ourselves. There is no immediate connection between her trade and ours, of this kind; they are separate and independent; and, of course, the incumbrances on the one would not injure the other. The superfluity of our products must be exported, to enable us to pay our debts to her; and we must submit to be loaded at her discretion. If we look forward to a period not far distant, we shall perceive that the productions of our country will infinitely exceed the demands which Great Britain and her connections can possibly have for them; and, as we shall then be greatly advanced in population, our wants will be proportionately increased. These circumstances will open an ample field for extortion and oppression.

The legislative authority of Parliament would always be ready to silence our murmurs by tyrannical edicts. These would be enforced by a formidable army, kept up among us for the purpose. The slightest struggles to recover our lost liberty would become dangerous, and even capital. Those hated things, Continental Conventions, by which there might be a communion of councils and measures, would be interdicted. Non-importation and non-exportation agreements would, in effect, be made *seditious, illegal,* and *treasonable.*[13] No remedy would be left, but in the clemency of our oppressors; a wretched one, indeed, and such as no prudent man would confide in! In whatever light we consider the matter, we shall find that we must effectually seal our bondage by adopting the mode you recommend.

Agreeably to your concessions, Great Britain is abundantly recompensed for the naval protection she affords, by the *principal profits* of our trade. It can therefore, with no color of justice, be urged upon us to permit her to raise a revenue through that channel.

But, after all, let us suppose that the emolument which arises from the simple and abstracted regulation of our trade is inadequate to the pro-

---

13. I believe these were the epithets bestowed on them by General Gage.

tection we derive from the parent State: does it follow that her just demands cannot be satisfied, unless we put it in her power to ruin us? When did the colonies refuse to contribute their proportion toward defraying the expenses of government? During the war our contributions were so liberal and generous that we were thought to have done more than our part, and restitution was accordingly made. Massachusetts, that injured, insulted, and calumniated country, was foremost in displaying its loyalty, and was parsimonious neither of its men nor money. But notwithstanding this no confidence, it seems, is due to our virtue or fidelity; but every thing is to be trusted to the wisdom and disinterestedness of a British Parliament.

We do not expect, nor require, that all should depend upon our integrity or generosity, but only a part; and this, every rule of equity entitles us to. We have assented to the exercise of a power which gives a certainty to Great Britain of a vast annual income; any further aids that may be necessary ought to be intrusted to our fidelity. When the circumstances of two parties will not admit of precise boundaries to the duty of each, it is not a dictate of justice to put one entirely into the power of the other. If the mother country would desist from grasping at too much, and permit us to enjoy the privileges of freemen, interest would concur with duty, and lead us to the performance of it. We should be sensible of the advantages of a mutual intercourse and connection, and should esteem the welfare of Britain as the best security for our own. She may, by kind treatment, secure our attachment in the powerful bands of self-interest. This is the conduct that prudence and sound policy point out; but, alas! to her own misfortune as well as ours, she is blind and infatuated.

If we take futurity into the account, as we no doubt ought to do, we shall find, that in fifty or sixty years, America will be in no need of protection from Great Britain. She will then be able to protect herself both at home and abroad. She will have a plenty of men, and a plenty of materials, to provide and equip a formidable navy. She will, indeed, owe a debt of gratitude to the parent State for past services; but the scale will then begin to turn in her favor; and the obligation for future services will be on the side of Great Britain. It will be the interest of the latter to keep us without a fleet, and, by this means, to continue to regulate our trade as before. But, in thus withholding the means of protection which we have within our own reach, she will chiefly consult her own advantage, and oblige herself much more than us. At that era, to enjoy the privilege of enriching herself by the direction of our commerce, and, at the same time, to derive supports, from our youthful vigor and strength, against all her enemies, and thereby to extend her conquests over them, will give her reason to bless the times that gave birth to these colonies.

By enlarging our views and turning our thoughts to future days, we must perceive that the special benefits we receive from the British nation are of a temporary and transient nature; while, on the other hand, those it may reap from us by an affectionate and parental conduct will be permanent and durable, and will serve to give it such a degree of stability and lasting prosperity as could not be expected in the common fluctuating course of human affairs. Such reflections will teach us that there is no propriety in making any concessions to Great Britain, which may be at all inconsistent with our safety.

You employ several contemptible artifices to varnish and recommend your scheme. Your conduct, in every respect, affords a striking instance of the depravity of human nature. You insinuate that the Pennsylvania Farmer* admits the right of Parliament to regulate our trade in the same sense you do. The very letter your extracts are taken from is expressly levelled against the revenue act, with regard to paper, glass, etc. The design of that, and all his subsequent papers, is to prove that all duties imposed upon the articles of commerce for the purpose of raising a rev-

---

* The reference here is to John Dickinson's "Letters from a Farmer in Pennsylvania to the Inhabitants of the British Colonies" (1768), reprinted in Merrill Jensen, ed., *Tracts of the American Revolution* (Bobbs-Merrill, 1967).

enue are to be considered in the same light as what you call *internal* taxes, and ought equally to be opposed.

By the "legal authority to regulate trade," he means nothing more than what the Congress have allowed: an authority to confine us to the use of our own manufactures; to prescribe our trade with foreign nations, and the like. This is the power he speaks of as being "lodged in the British Parliament." And as to *general duties,* he means such as the people of Great Britain are to pay as well as ourselves. Duties, for the purpose of a revenue raised upon us only he calls *special* duties, and says: "They are as much a tax upon us as those imposed by the Stamp Act."

The following passage will show the sentiments of this ingenious and worthy gentleman and at the same time will serve to illustrate what I have heretofore said.

"If you once admit," says he, "that Great Britain may lay duties upon her exportations to us, *for the purpose of levying money on us only,* she will then have nothing to do, but to lay duties on the articles which she prohibits us to manufacture, and the tragedy of *American* liberty is finished. We have been prohibited from procuring manufactures, in all cases, anywhere but from Great Britain (excepting linens, which we are permitted to import directly from Ireland). We have been prohibited in some cases from manufacturing for ourselves, and may be prohibited in others. We are therefore exactly in the situation of a city besieged, which is surrounded by the besiegers in every part but *one.* If that is closed up no step can be taken, *but to surrender at discretion.* If Great Britain can order us to come to her for the necessaries we want, and can order us to pay what taxes she pleases before we take them away, or when we land them here, we are as abject slaves as *France* and *Poland* can show, in wooden shoes, and with uncombed hair.[14]

"Perhaps the nature of the necessities of dependent States, caused by the policy of a governing one for her own benefit, may be elucidated by

---

14. The peasants of *France* wear wooden shoes; and the vassals of *Poland* are remarkable for matted hair which never can be combed.

a fact mentioned in history. When the Carthaginians were possessed of the island of *Sardinia,* they made a decree that the Sardinians should not raise *corn,* nor get it any other way than from the *Carthaginians.* Then, by imposing any duties they would upon it, they drained from the miserable *Sardinians* any sums they pleased; and whenever that miserable and oppressed people made the least movement to assert their liberty, their tyrants starved them to death or submission. This may be called the most perfect kind of political necessity."*

You would persuade us also that Mr. *Pitt's* sentiments accord with yours, about the regulation of trade; but this is as false as the other. When he tells them "to exercise every power but that of taking money out of our pockets," he does not mean that they shall barely refrain from a *manual operation* upon our pockets; but they shall exact money from us in no way whatsoever. To tax the commodities Great Britain obliges us to take from her only is as much taking money out of our pockets as to tax our estates, and must be equally excluded by Mr. Pitt's prohibition.

You all along argue upon a supposititious denial of the right of Parliament to regulate our trade. You tell us: "It will never give up the right of regulating the trade of the colonies"; and, in another place: "If we succeed in depriving Great Britain of the power of regulating our trade, the colonies will probably be soon at variance with each other. Their commercial interests will interfere;[15] there will be no supreme power to interpose; and discord and animosity must ensue."

I leave others to determine whether you are more defective in memory or honesty: but in order to show that you are starting difficulties where there are really none, I will transcribe, for your perusal, part of the fourth resolve of the Congress. After asserting the right of the several provincial legislatures to an exclusive power of legislation "in all cases of taxation and internal policy," they conclude thus: "But from the necessity of the

---

* The quotation is from Dickinson, "Letter II," in Jensen, *Tracts,* 138–39.

15. I do not see any reason to believe this would be the case; but as it is of no importance to controvert it, I shall pass it over.

case, and a regard to the mutual interests of both countries, we cheerfully consent to the operation of such acts of the British Parliament, as are *bona fide* restrained to *the regulation of our external commerce,* for the purpose of securing the commercial advantages of the whole empire to the mother country, and the commercial benefits of its respective members; excluding every idea of taxation, internal or external, for raising a revenue on the subjects in America without their consent."

It seems to me not impossible that our trade may be so regulated as to prevent the discord and animosity, at the prospect of which you are so terrified, without the least assistance from a *revenue.*

Thus have I not only disproved the existence of that parliamentary authority of which you are so zealous an abettor, but also shown that the mode you have proposed for the accommodation of our disputes would be destructive to American freedom. My next business is to vindicate the Congress by a few natural inferences, and such reflections on the state of our commercial connection with the mother country as are necessary to show the insignificancy of your objections to my former arguments on this head.

Since it has been proved, that the British Parliament has no right either to the legislation or taxation of America, and since neither could be ceded without betraying our liberties, the Congress would have acted inconsistent with their duty to their country had they done it. Their conduct, therefore, so far from being reprehensible, was perfectly justifiable and laudable.

The regulation of our trade, in the sense it is now admitted, is the only power we can, with justice to ourselves, permit the British Parliament to exercise; and it is a privilege of so important a nature, so beneficial and lucrative to Great Britain, that she ought, in equity, to be contented with it, and not attempt to grasp at any thing more. The Congress, therefore, have made the only concession which the welfare and prosperity of America would warrant, or which Great Britain, in reason, could expect.

All your clamors, therefore, against them for not having drawn some proper line are groundless and ridiculous. They have drawn the only line which American freedom will authorize, or which the relation between the parent state and the colonies requires.

It is a necessary consequence, and not an assumed point, that the claim of Parliament to *bind us by statutes in all cases whatsoever* is unconstitutional, unjust, and tyrannical; and the repeated attempts to carry it into execution evince a fixed, inveterate design to exterminate the liberties of America.

Mr. Grenville, during his administration, was the projector of this scheme. His conduct, as a minister, has been severely arraigned by his successors in office, and by the nation in general; but, notwithstanding this, a measure which disgraces his character more than any thing else has been steadily pursued ever since.

The Stamp Act was the commencement of our misfortunes; which, in consequence of the *spirited* opposition made by us, was repealed. The Revenue Act, imposing duties on paper, glass, etc., came next, and was also partly repealed on the same account. A part, however, was left to be the instrument of some future attack. The present minister, in conjunction with a mercenary tribe of merchants, attempted to effect, by stratagem, what could not be done by an open, undisguised manner of proceeding. His emissaries, everywhere, were set to work. They endeavored, by every possible device, to allure us into the snare. The act, passed for the purpose, was misrepresented; and we were assured, with all the parade of pretended patriotism, that our liberties were in no danger. The advantage we should receive from the probable cheapness of English tea was played off with every exaggeration of falsehood, and specious declamations on the criminality of illicit trade served as a gilding for the whole. Thus truth and its opposite were blended. The men who could make just reflections on the sanctity of an oath were yet base enough to strike at the vitals of those rights which ought to be held sacred by every rational being.

It so happened that the first tea ship arrived at Boston. The Assembly of that province, justly alarmed at the consequences, made repeated applications to the consignees for the East India Company, requesting them to send back the tea. They as often refused to comply. The ship was detained till the time was elapsed; after which the tea must have been landed, and the duties paid, or it would have been seized by the Custom-House. To prevent this, a part of the citizens of Boston assembled, proceeded to the ship, and threw the tea into the river.[16]

The scheme of the ministry was disappointed on all hands. The tea was returned from all the colonies except South Carolina. It was landed there; but such precautions were taken as equally served to baffle their attempt.

This abortion of their favorite plan, inflamed the ministerial ire. They breathed nothing but vengeance against America. Menaces of punishment resounded through both Houses of Parliament. The Commons of Great Britain spoke more in the supercilious tone of masters than in the becoming language of fellow-subjects. To all the judicious reasonings of a Burke, or Barré, no other answer was returned than the idle tale of *lenity* and *severity*. Much was said on their past forbearance, and of their future resentment. This was the burthen of the song. The Quixote minister, too, promised to bring America to his feet. Humiliating idea, and such as ought to be spurned by every free-born American!

Boston was the first victim to the meditated vengeance. An act was passed to block up her ports and destroy her commerce, with every aggravating circumstance that can be imagined. It was not left at her option to elude the stroke by paying for the tea; but she was also to make such satisfaction to the officers of his Majesty's revenue, and others who might have suffered, as should be judged *reasonable by the governor.*

Nor is this all. Before her commerce could be restored, she must have submitted to the authority claimed and exercised by the Parliament.[17]

---

16. I shall examine the justice and policy of this procedure in some future publication.

17. This must be evident to every person who has read the act. The prefatory part of it is in these words: "Whereas, dangerous commotions and insurrections have been fomented and raised in the town of Boston, etc.; in which commotions and insurrections,

Had the rest of America passively looked on while a sister colony was subjugated, the same fate would gradually have overtaken all. The safety of the whole depends upon the mutual protection of every part. If the sword of oppression be permitted to lop off one limb without opposition, reiterated strokes will soon dismember the whole body. Hence, it was the duty and interest of all the colonies to succor and support the one which was suffering. It is sometimes sagaciously urged, that we ought to commiserate the distresses of the people of Massachusetts, but not intermeddle in their affairs, so far as perhaps to bring ourselves into like circumstances with them. This might be good reasoning, if our neutrality would not be more dangerous than our participation; but I am unable to conceive how the colonies in general would have any security against oppression, if they were once to content themselves with barely *pitying* each other, while Parliament was prosecuting and enforcing its demands.

---

certain valuable cargoes of tea, etc., were seized and destroyed: And whereas, in the present condition of the said town and harbor, the commerce of his Majesty's subjects cannot be safely carried on there, nor the *customs* payable to his Majesty duly collected," etc.

The commotions specified are those in which the tea was destroyed; the commerce obstructed was that of the East India Company; and the customs which could not be collected were those on the tea. These are the evils the act is intended to punish and remove; accordingly it provides that "whenever it shall appear to his Majesty, in his privy council, that peace and obedience to the laws (*i.e.,* the laws of Parliament) shall be so far restored in the said town of Boston that the trade of Great Britain may safely be carried on there, and his Majesty's *customs* duly collected," then his Majesty may, at his discretion, so far open the port as to him seems necessary. So that until the Bostonians shall submit to let the trade of Great Britain be carried on upon her own terms, and suffer his Majesty's customs (the duty upon tea, or any other Parliament may impose) to be duly collected, they must remain in their present distressed situation: that is, unless they resign their freedom and put on the ignominious yoke tendered them by Parliament, they are never to recover their lost trade. Hence it appears how weak, ungenerous, and contemptible that objection is, which supposes the Bostonians might have avoided their present calamities by paying for the tea. The truth is, they had no alternative but submission to all the *unjust claims of Parliament.*

Unless they continually protect and assist each other, they must all inevitably fall a prey to their enemies.

Extraordinary emergencies require extraordinary expedients. The best mode of opposition was that in which there might be a union of councils. This was necessary to ascertain the boundaries of our rights, and to give weight and dignity to our measures, both in Great Britain and America. A Congress was accordingly proposed, and universally agreed to.

You, sir, triumph in the supposed *illegality* of this body: but granting your supposition were true, it would be a matter of no real importance. When the first principles of civil society are violated, and the rights of a whole people are invaded, the common forms of municipal law are not to be regarded. Men may then betake themselves to the law of nature; and, if they but conform their actions to that standard, all cavils against them betray either ignorance or dishonesty. There are some events in society, to which human laws cannot extend, but when applied to them, lose all their force and efficacy. In short, when human laws contradict or discountenance the means which are necessary to preserve the essential rights of any society, they defeat the proper end of all laws, and so become null and void.

But you have barely asserted, not proved, this *illegality*. If by the term you mean a contrariety to law, I desire you to produce the law against it. I maintain there is none in being. If you mean that there is no law, the intention of which may authorize such a convention, I deny this also. It has been always a principle of the law, that subjects have a right to state their grievances, and petition the king for redress. This is explicitly acknowledged by the act of the first of William and Mary; and "all prosecutions and commitments for such petitioning" are declared to be illegal. So far, then, the Congress was a body founded in law; for if subjects have such a right, they may undoubtedly elect and depute persons from among themselves to act for them.[18]

18. All lawyers agree that the *spirit* and *reason* of a law is one of the principal rules of interpretation; if so, it cannot be doubted that when a people are aggrieved, and their

As to the particular agreements entered into with respect to our commerce, the law makes no provision for or against them; they are perfectly indifferent in a legal sense. We may or may not trade, as is most suitable to our own circumstances.

The deputies chosen in the several provinces met at Philadelphia according to appointment, and framed a set of resolves declarative of the rights of America; all which I have by general arguments proved are consonant to reason and nature, to the spirit of the British Constitution, and to the intention of our charters. They made the only concession (as I have also shown) that their duty to themselves and their country would justify, or that the connection between Great Britain and the colonies demanded.

They solicited the king for a redress of grievances, but justly concluding from past experience, from the behavior and declarations of the majority in both Houses of Parliament, and from the known character and avowed designs of the minister, that little or no dependence was to be placed upon bare entreaties, they thought it necessary to second them by restrictions on trade.

In my former defence of the measures of the Congress, I proved, in a manner you never will be able to invalidate, that petitions and remonstrances would certainly be unavailing. I will now examine your frivolous and prevaricating reply.

You answer thus: "In the commotions occasioned by the Stamp Act, we referred to petitions and remonstrances; our grievances were pointed out, and redress solicited with temper and decency. They were heard; they were attended to; and the disagreeable act repealed. The same mode of application succeeded with regard to the duties laid upon glass, painters' colors, etc. You say, indeed, that our addresses on this occasion were treated with contempt and neglected. But, I beseech you, were not our addresses received, read, and debated upon? And was not the repeal of

---

circumstances will not allow them unitedly to petition in their own persons, they may appoint representatives to do it for them.

those acts the consequence? *The fact you know is as I state it.* If these acts were not only disagreeable to the Americans, but were also found to militate against the commercial interests of Great Britain, it proves what I asserted above; that duties which injure our trade will soon be felt in England, and then there will be no difficulty in getting them repealed."

I entirely deny the fact to be as you state it; and you are conscious it is not. Our addresses were not heard, attended to, and the disagreeable act repealed in consequence of them. If this had been the case, why was no notice taken of them in the repealing act? Why were not our complaints assigned as the inducement to it? On the contrary, these are the express words of the first repeal, to which the second is also similar: "Whereas the continuance of the said act would be attended *with many inconveniences,* and *may be productive of consequences greatly detrimental to the commercial interests of Great Britain:* May it therefore please your most excellent Majesty, by and with the advice and consent, etc., that from and after the first day of May, 1766, the above-mentioned act, and the several matters and things therein contained, shall be, and is, and are, hereby repealed and made void, to all intents and purposes whatsoever."

The inconveniences and the ill consequences to Great Britain are the only reasons given for the revolution of the act. How then can you pretend to say it was in compliance with our petitions? You must think the complaisance of your readers very great to imagine they will credit your assertions at the expense of their own understandings.

Neither is the use you make of the assigned reasons at all just. The consequences, so detrimental to the commercial interests of Great Britain, are not such as would have resulted from the natural operation of the act, had it been submitted to; but from the opposition made by us, and the cessation of imports which had taken place.

A non-importation (to which you have so violent an aversion) was the only thing that procured us redress on preceding occasions. We did not formerly, any more than now, confine ourselves to petitions only, but took care to adopt a more prevailing method; to wit—a suspension of trade.

But what proves to a demonstration that our former petitions were unsuccessful is, that the grand object they aimed at was never obtained. This was an exemption from parliamentary taxation. Our addresses turned entirely upon this point. And so far were they from succeeding, that immediately upon the repeal of the Stamp Act, a subsequent act was passed, declaring the right of Parliament to bind us by statutes in all cases whatsoever. This declaration of the unlimited, universal authority of Parliament, was a direct denial of the leading claim held up in our petition, and of course a rejection of the petition itself.

The same observations are applicable to the Revenue Act, which, had our addresses been successful, would have been wholly, not partially, revoked; and we should not, at this time, have had any occasion to renew our complaints, but should have been in a state of security and tranquillity.

In my former reflections on this head, I urged many considerations to show that there is less reason now than ever to expect deliverance by means of remonstrance and entreaty. And, indeed, if we consider the vindictive spirit diffused through the words and actions of our oppressors, we must be convinced of this. It impeaches the understandings of the ministry and the Parliament in the grossest manner, to suppose they have renewed their attempts, and taken such violent methods to carry them into execution, merely to have the pleasure of undoing the whole, in condescension to our prayers and complaints. The taxation of America is an object too near at heart to be resigned unless from necessity; and if they would not have abandoned the principle, there could be no reason to expect they would have desisted from the exercise of it in the present instance. For the duty on tea is in itself very trifling; and, since that is opposed, they could not hope to vary the mode in any way that would be less offensive and less obnoxious to opposition.

In answer to the instance I produced from the unsuccessful application of the Boston Assembly, you tell me that "the governor against whom the complaint was made was called to a public trial before the only court where the cause was cognizable, the King in Council, but the Boston

Assembly could not support their charge, and the governor was acquitted." The truth is, their charge was extremely well supported in the eye
of strict justice, but it was destitute of the mere formalities of law, and
on this score it was rejected. They accused him of treachery and falsehood, and produced his own letters against him. It was not admitted as
a *legal* charge, or *crimen;* nor the party's letters as an evidence, or *testis;*
and by these evasions the criminal escaped the punishment he deserved,
and instead of it, has been advanced to higher honors, while the com-
plainants were unrelieved and insulted. I remember when the particulars
of this transaction were first published, there was one circumstance mentioned: that the petition in question was pronounced at *St. James'* to be
"*a seditious, vexatious,* and *scandalous libel.*"

You tell me: "There is also this reason why we should, at least, have
tried the mode of petition and remonstrance, to obtain a removal of the
grievances we complain of,—the friends of America and England have
strongly recommended it as the most decent and probable means of succeeding." I wish you had been so kind as to have particularized those
friends you speak of. I am inclined to believe you would have found some
difficulty in this. There have been some publications in the newspapers,
said to be extracts of letters from England; but who are the authors of
them? How do you know they were not written in America? or, if they
came from England, that the writers of them were really sincere friends?
I have heard one or two persons named as the authors of some of these
letters; but they were those whose sincerity we have the greatest reason
to distrust. The general tenor of advice from those with whose integrity
we are best acquainted, has been, to place no dependence on the justice
or clemency of Great Britain, but to work our deliverance by a spirited
and self-denying opposition. Restrictions on our trade have been expressly pointed out and recommended as the only probable source of
redress.

You say: "If the information from England be true, we have by our
haughty demands detached most of our friends there from our interest,
and forced them to take part against us." Pray, sir, where did you get this

information? Is there any inhabitant of the invisible world that brings intelligence to you in a supernatural way? There have been no arrivals from England preceding the time you wrote your letter, that have brought any account of the proceedings of the Congress being received there, or of the consequences resulting from them. Your information must have either come to you in a miraculous manner, or it must be a fiction of your own imagination.

But there are other powerful reasons against trusting to petitions only, in our present circumstances. The town of Boston is in a very critical situation. Men, under sufferings, are extremely apt, either to plunge into desperation, or to grow disheartened and dejected. If the colonies, in general, appear remiss, or unwilling to adopt vigorous measures, in order to procure the most speedy relief, the people of Massachusetts might perhaps have been hurried on to a rash and fatal conduct, or they might have become languid and lifeless. Delays are extremely dangerous in affairs of such vast consequence.

The dispute might have been spun out by ministerial artifice, till the generality of the people became careless and negligent, and, of course, fitter to be imposed upon, and less forward to assert their rights with firmness and spirit. THE HAND OF BRIBERY MIGHT HAVE BEEN STRETCHED ACROSS THE ATLANTIC, and the number of domestic vipers increased among us. The ministry and their agents here are active and subtile; nothing would have been neglected that might have a tendency to deceive the ignorant and unwary, or to attract the dishonest and avaricious. How great an influence places, pensions, and honors have upon the minds of men, we may easily discover, by contrasting the former with the present conduct of some among ourselves. Many who, at the time of the Stamp Act, were loudest in the cause of liberty, and the most ardent promoters of the spirited proceedings on that occasion, have now, from patriots of the first magnitude, dwindled into *moderate men,* friends to order and good government, dutiful and zealous servants to the ministry.

Had our petitions failed, we should have found our difficulties multiplied much more than we can imagine; and since there was the highest probability of a failure, it would have been madness to have hazarded so much upon so unpromising a footing.

It betrays an ignorance of human nature to suppose that a design formed and ripened for several years against the liberties of any people, might be frustrated by the mere force of entreaty. Men must cease to be as fond of power as they are before this can be the case.

I therefore infer that if the Congress had not concerted other, more efficacious measures, they would have trifled away the liberties of their country, and merited censure instead of approbation. Commercial regulations were the only peaceable means from which we could have the least hope of success. These they have entered into; and these, I maintain, must succeed, if they are not treacherously or pusillanimously infringed.

You tell me, "I overrate the importance of these colonies to the British empire"; and proceed to make such assertions as must convince every intelligent person that you are either a mortal foe to truth or totally ignorant of the matter you undertake. The following extracts will show whether my representations have been just or not.

"Our plantations spend mostly our *English* manufactures—and those of *all sorts* almost imaginable, in *prodigious* quantities; and employ near *two thirds* of all our English shipping; so that we have more people in *England,* by reason of our plantations in *America.*[19]

"We may safely advance, that our trade and navigation are *greatly* increased by our colonies, and that they really are a source of treasure and naval power to this kingdom, since they *work for us,* and their treasure *centres here.* Before their settlement, *our manufactures were few,* and those but *indifferent;* the number of English merchants very small; and the *whole shipping* of the nation much inferior to what now belongs to the northern colonies only. *These are certain facts.* But since their establish-

19. Postlethwait. [The reference is to Malachy Postlethwayt, *The Universal Dictionary of Trade and Commerce, Translated from the French of Monsieur Savary: with large additions and improvements,* 2nd ed., 2 vols. (London, 1757).]

ment, our condition has altered for the better, *almost to a degree beyond credibility*. Our manufactures are *prodigiously* increased, chiefly by the demand for them in the plantations, where they *at least take off one half*, and supply us with many valuable commodities for exportation, which is as great emolument to the mother kingdom as to the plantations themselves."[20]

The same author says, in another place: "Before the settlement of these colonies, our *manufactures were few*, and those but indifferent. In those days, we had, not only our *naval stores*, but our *ships*, from our neighbors."

"I shall sum up my whole remarks," says another writer, "on our *American* colonies, with this observation: that, as they are a *certain* annual revenue of *several millions sterling* to their mother country, they ought carefully to be protected, duly encouraged, and every opportunity that presents improved for their increment and advantage; *as every one they can possibly reap, must at last return to us with interest*."[21]

These quotations clearly prove that the colonies are of the last importance to Great Britain. They not only take off vast quantities of her manufactures, but furnish her with materials to extend her trade with foreign nations. They also supply her with naval stores, and, in a great measure, with a navy itself. The present flourishing state of her commerce, is chiefly to be attributed to the colonies who *work for her*, and whose treasure *centres in her*. How unjust, therefore, is it in her not to be satisfied with the advantages she has hitherto received from us, but to aim at depriving us of our freedom and happiness! And what ruinous consequences must flow from a cessation of our trade, on which her manufactures so much depend! What prodigious numbers must be thrown out of employ and reduced to beggary and misery!

"But she is a great nation; has vast resources; may easily supply the want of our trade by making very small concessions to Portugal, Russia,

---

20. *Ibid.*

21. *Les mercatoria.* [The quotation is from *Lex Mercatoria Rediviva: or, The Merchant's Directory* (London, 1761).]

Turkey, etc. Should our non-importation distress her manufactures, every man may employ himself to labor on a farm; and the price of grain would be much advanced in France, Spain, and the Mediterranean. Notwithstanding the present high cultivation of the lands in England, that kingdom is capable of being improved, by agriculture and commerce, so as to maintain double the number of people that it does at present. The improvements in Scotland within the last thirty years are amazing. The enterprising spirit of the people has opened an easy intercourse between all parts of the country, and they have been enriched by commerce to a surprising degree."

I can hardly prevail upon myself to give a serious answer to such ridiculous rant; but it may be requisite for the sake of the uninformed, and of course it would be improper to decline it.

The national debt is now about one hundred and forty millions sterling—a debt unparalleled in the annals of any country besides. The surplus of the annual revenues, after paying the interest of this debt, and the usual expenses of the nation, is upon an average about one million and a quarter sterling;[22] so that with all their present resources they would not be able to discharge the public debt in less than *one hundred and twelve years,* should the peace continue all that time. It is well known that most of the necessaries of life are at present heavily taxed in Great Britain and Ireland. The common people are extremely impoverished, and find it very difficult to procure a subsistence. They are totally unable to bear any new impositions; and of course there can be no new internal sources opened. These are stubborn facts, and notorious to every person that has the least acquaintance with the situation of the two kingdoms. Had there been the vast resources you speak of, why have they not been improved to exonerate the people and discharge the enormous debt of the nation? The guardians of the state have been a supine, negligent, and stupid pack indeed, to have overlooked, in the manner they have done,

22. See a calculation made by Blackstone. He says, the year '65, two millions were paid, and three millions in the succeeding years; *i.e.,* five millions in four years.

those numerous expedients they might have fallen upon for the relief of the public. It cannot be expected but that a war will take place in the course of a few years, if not immediately; and then, through the negligence of her rulers, Great Britain, already tottering under her burthens, will be obliged to increase them till they become altogether insupportable, and she must sink under the weight of them. These considerations render it very evident that the mighty resources you set forth in such pompous terms have nothing but an *imaginary* existence, or they would not have been left so uncultivated in such necessitous and pressing circumstances.

You think you have nothing to do but to mention the names of a few countries, Portugal, Russia, Turkey, etc., and you have found out an easy remedy for the inconveniences flowing from the loss of our trade. Yet in truth Great Britain carries on as extensive a commerce with those countries, and all others, as their circumstances will permit. Her trade is upon the decline with many of them. France has in a great measure supplanted her in Spain, Portugal, and Turkey, and is continually gaining ground. Russia is increasing her own manufactures fast; and the demand for those of Great Britain must decrease in proportion.

"Most of the nations of Europe have interfered with *her,* more or less, in divers of her *staple manufactures,* within half a century; not only in her woollen, but in her lead and tin manufactures, as well as her fisheries."[23]

A certain writer in England, who has written on the present situation of affairs with great temper, deliberation, and apparent integrity, has these observations: "The condition of the great *staple manufactures* of our country is well known; those of the linen and the silk are in the greatest distress, and the woollen and the linen are now publicly bandied and contending against one another. One part of our people is starving at home on the alms of their parishes, and another running abroad to this very country that we are contending with. The produce of North America, that used to be sent yearly to Great Britain, is reckoned at about four

23. Postlethwait.

millions sterling; the manufactures of Great Britain, and other commodities returned from hence, at nearly the same sum; the debts due from America to British merchants here at about six millions, or a year and a half of that commerce. Supposing, therefore, the Americans to act in this case as they did in the time of the Stamp Act; we shall then have yearly, until the final settlement of this affair, manufactures to the value of four millions sterling, left and heaped on the hands of our merchants and master manufacturers; or we shall have workmen and poor people put out of employ and turned adrift in that proportion. There will likewise be drawn from our home consumption, and out of our general trade and traffic, North American commodities to the same value; and debts, to the immense sums above mentioned, will be withheld from private people here. What effects these things will produce, considering the present state of our trade, manufactures, and manufacturers, the condition of our poor at home, and the numbers of people running abroad, it don't want many words to explain and set forth. *They were before severely felt* for the time that they lasted, and it is apprehended that the present situation of the public is yet more liable to the impression. These are some of the difficulties and distresses which we are, for a trial of skill, going to bring on ourselves, and which will be perpetually magnifying and increasing as long as the unnatural contest shall continue."*

From these facts and authorities it appears unquestionable, that the trade of Great Britain, instead of being capable of improvement among foreign countries, is rather declining; and instead of her being able to bear the loss of our commerce, she stands in need of more colonies to consume her manufactures.

It is idle to talk of employing those who might be thrown out of business upon farms. All the lands in England, of any value, have been long ago disposed of, and are already cultivated as high as possible. The

* Baron Rokeby, *Considerations on the Measures Carrying on with respect to the British Colonies in North America . . .* (London: Printed. Boston, reprinted and sold by Edes and Gill, in Queen-Street, 1774), 29–30.

laborious farmers find it an exceeding difficult task to pay their yearly taxes and supply their families with the bare necessaries of life; and it would be impracticable to give employment in agriculture to any more than are already engaged. We can have no doubt of this, if we consider the small extent of territory of Great Britain, the antiquity of its settlement, and the vast number of people it contains. It is rather overstocked with inhabitants; and were it not for its extensive commerce, it could not maintain near the number it does at present. This is acknowledged on all hands. None but yourself would hazard the absurdity of a denial. The emigrations from Great Britain, particularly from the north part of it, as well as the most authentic accounts, prove the contrary of your representations. Men are generally too much attached to their native country to leave it, and dissolve all their connections, unless they are driven to it by necessity. The swarms that every year come over to America, will never suffer any reasonable man to believe, upon the strength of your word, that the people in Scotland, or Ireland are even in tolerable circumstances.

I cannot forbear wondering, when you talk of the price of grain being advanced in France, Spain, and the Mediterranean, and insinuate that Great Britain may be able to supply them. It will be well if she can raise grain enough for herself, so as not to feel the want of those considerable quantities she frequently gets from us. I am apt to think she will experience some inconveniences on this account.

With respect to Ireland you think yourself under no obligation to point out where she may find purchasers for her linens so numerous and wealthy as we are; but unless you could do this, you must leave that country in very deplorable circumstances. It is not true, that she may do just as well with her linens upon her hands, as we can with our flaxseed upon ours. Linen is a staple manufacture of hers, and the sole means of subsistence to a large part of her inhabitants. Flaxseed, as an article of commerce, is comparatively of little importance to us; but we shall stand in need of all the flax we can raise, to manufacture linens for ourselves, and therefore shall not lose our seed by ceasing to export it. I shall say more of this hereafter.

Nor is it by any means a just inference, that because Ireland formerly subsisted without a linen manufactory, she would not, therefore, severely feel any present obstruction to the sale of the article in question. Her burthens are now much more grievous than they formerly were; and of course her resources ought to be proportionately greater, or she must sink under the pressure of them. The linen manufactory is, at this time, one of her most valuable resources, and could not be materially injured or impeded without producing the most melancholy effects. The distressed condition of Ireland will not admit of any diminution of her *means*, but pressingly demands an enlargement of them.

It is of little moment to contest the possibility that that country might procure a sufficiency of flax elsewhere than from us, till it can be shown where she may find a mart for her linens equal to the American; and this you are not willing even to attempt. Yet I have credible information that she could not obtain from Holland much more than usual (for the reasons I before assigned), and that she has always had as much from the Baltic as she could conveniently get. With regard to Canada, any considerable supply from thence would be a work of time, and no relief to her immediate exigencies.

I observed, in my former pamphlet, that "the Dutch may withhold their usual supplies; they may choose to improve the occasion for the advancement of their own trade; they may take advantage of the scarcity of materials in Ireland to increase and put off their own manufactures." You answer it by saying: "You never yet knew a Hollander who would withhold any thing that would fetch him a good price." The force of my observation turns upon its being his interest to do it. You should have shown, that it would be more profitable to him to sell it to the Irish than to retain it for the purposes mentioned; otherwise, that very avarice you ascribe to him will operate as I supposed.

You are unmercifully witty upon what I said concerning the West Indies; but the misfortune of it is, you have done nothing else than "blunder round about my meaning." I will endeavor to explain myself in a manner more level to your capacity.

The lands in the West Indies are extremely valuable, because they produce the sugar-cane, which is a very lucrative plant; but they are small in quantity, and therefore their proprietors appropriate only small portions to the purpose of raising food. They are very populous, and therefore the food raised among themselves goes but little way. They could not afford sufficient sustenance to their inhabitants, unless they were chiefly or entirely applied to the production of necessaries; because they are so small in quantity, and so thickly inhabited.

These are truths which every person acquainted with the West Indies must acquiesce in; and should they be deprived of external succors, they must either starve or suspend the cultivation of the sugarcane. The latter is the better side of the dilemma, but that would cut off an annual income of several millions sterling to Great Britain; for it cannot admit of a doubt, that the chief part of the profits of the English West Indies ultimately centres there.

But, in order to disappoint my malice, you tell me that Canada raises four hundred thousand bushels of wheat a year; and this, you imagine, will pretty well supply the wants of the West Indies. But give me leave to inform you, that it would not satisfy a tenth part of them. The single island of Jamaica would require much more. At a moderate computation, I believe there are four hundred thousand people in the British West Indies only. Let us allow a pound of wheat a day, upon an average, to each,[24] and make a calculation accordingly.

At a pound a day, every person must be supposed to consume three hundred and sixty-five pounds a year; that is, about twelve bushels. Now, as there are as many people as there are bushels of wheat raised in Canada, and as each person would consume twelve bushels, it follows that the quantity you mention would not be above a twelfth part sufficient.

But can we imagine that all the wheat of Canada would be devoted to the use of the British West Indies? If our ports were to be blocked

24. This allowance cannot be thought too much, if we consider that the negroes live chiefly upon grain, and must continue to do so, because the quantity of flesh and fish would be proportionably diminished when our supplies failed.

up, would not the French and Spanish islands be in great distress for provisions? And have not the Canadians any near connections among them? Would they not naturally sympathize with them, and do all in their power to afford relief? And could they find no means to accomplish their inclinations? To answer these questions is easy. The islands belonging to the French and Spaniards will be greatly distressed; the Canadians will be very ready and desirous to assist them; and they will contrive some expedients to communicate a large share of what their country yields.

What you say concerning the lumber exported from Canada is totally false. That country labors under many inconveniences which have hitherto prevented the exportation of that article, but in very small quantities, and of a particular kind. The places where the lumber grows are so far distant from the seaports that the expense of transportation is too great to make it worth while to ship any other than butt staves, and these must be brought quite from Lake Champlain. This disadvantage, together with the number of hands it would require, and the time necessary to enter extensively into any branch of trade, and to remove all the impediments naturally in the way, would render the situation of the West Indies truly pitiable, were they once necessitated to depend upon Canada only, for supplies of lumber.

The attention of Mississippi is entirely engrossed in raising corn and indigo. The advantage arising from these articles is much greater than would result from lumber; and of course the people of that country will never attend to the latter in preference to the former.

Thus have I proved, in a full, clear, and conclusive manner, that a cessation of our trade with Great Britain, Ireland, and the West Indies would be productive of the most fatal consequences to them all; and that, therefore, the peace, happiness, and safety of the British empire are connected with the redress of our grievances; and, if they are at all consulted, our measures cannot fail of success.

As to the justice of proceeding in the manner we have done, it must depend upon the *necessity* of such a mode of conduct. If the British

Parliament are claiming and exercising an unjust authority, we are right in opposing it by every necessary means. If remonstrances and petitions have been heretofore found ineffectual (and we have no reasonable ground to expect the contrary at present), it is prudent and justifiable to try other methods, and these can only be restrictions on trade. Our duty to ourselves and posterity supersedes the duties of benevolence to our fellow-subjects in Great Britain, Ireland, and the West Indies.

You can never confute the arguments I before made use of on this head, unless you can prove the right of Parliament to act as it has done, or the likelihood of succeeding by petitions. Your feeble endeavors to effect this, I have sufficiently baffled. You must now collect new forces and make a more vigorous effort, or you must quit the field in disgrace.

Such vociferation as this is not to be admitted instead of argument: "Are the Irish and the West Indians accountable for our mad freaks? Do you expect to extend the tyranny of the Congress over the whole British empire, by the legerdemain of calling it American freedom? Do you think that the Irish and West Indians are in duty bound to enter into our non-importation, non-consumption, and non-exportation agreements, till our grievances, real or pretended, are removed? And that they deserve to be starved if they do not? Enjoy your folly and malevolence if you can."

The resistance[25] we are making to parliamentary tyranny cannot wear the aspect of *mad freaks* to any but such mad imaginations as yours. It will be deemed virtuous and laudable by every ingenuous mind. When I said that the people of Great Britain, Ireland, and the West Indies were to be considered as *politically* criminal for remaining neutral while our privateers were attacked, I did not mean that they ought to enter into any of the above-mentioned agreements, but that it was their duty to signify in a public manner their disapprobation of the measures carrying on, and to use all their influence to have them laid aside. Had they

---

25. I mean the general resistance. That there have been some irregularities committed in America I freely confess. It would be miraculous and inconsistent with human nature for a people in such critical and trying circumstances to act perfectly right.

interested themselves in the affair with any degree of zeal and earnestness, we should not probably have had occasion to act as we do, and they would not have been in danger of their present calamities. Their obligation to assist us in the preservation of our rights is of the very same nature with ours to carry on a trade with them.

But you insist upon it, we should not be able to live without the manufactures of Great Britain, and that we should be ruined by a prohibition of our exports. "The first winter after our English goods are consumed we shall be starving with cold"; after all our endeavors, "the requisite quantity of wool to clothe the inhabitants of this continent could not be obtained in twenty years." As to cotton, it "must come from the Southern colonies; and the expense of bringing it by land would be too great for the poor. Besides, we have nobody to manufacture our materials after we have got them." All these, you think, are insuperable obstacles, and would, if duly considered, induce us to bend our necks tamely and quietly to the proffered yoke, as much less dreadful than the evils attendant upon our measures will inevitably be.

Nature has disseminated her blessings variously throughout this continent. Some parts of it are favorable to some things, others to others; some colonies are best calculated for grain, others for flax and hemp, others for cotton, and others for live stock of every kind. By this means a mutually advantageous intercourse may be established between them all. If we were to turn our attention from external to internal commerce, we should give greater stability and more lasting prosperity to our country than she can possibly have otherwise. We should not then import the luxuries and vices of foreign climes; nor should we make such hasty strides to public corruption and depravity.

Let all those lands which are rich enough to produce flax and hemp be applied to that purpose; and let such parts as have been a long time settled still continue to be appropriated to grain, or other things they are fit for. We shall want as much of the former articles as can be raised, and perhaps as much of the latter as may be requisite toward the due improvement of the poorer part of our soil. Let it be considered that the colonies which are adapted to the production of materials for manufactures will not be employed in raising grain, but must take what they use chiefly from the other colonies, and, in return, supply their materials. By this means, and by dedicating no more of our land to the raising of wheat, rye, corn, etc., than is incapable of producing other things, we shall find no superfluity of those articles, and shall make a very beneficial use of all our lands. This is practicable; difficulties may be started, but none which perseverance and industry may not overcome.

The clothes we already have in use, and the goods at present in the country, will, with care, be sufficient to last *three years.*[26] During that time we shall be increasing our sheep as much as possible. It is unfair to judge of the future from the past. Hitherto we have paid no great attention to them; we have killed and exported as fast as we could obtain a sale. When we come to attend properly to the matter, to kill but few and to export none, we shall, in the course of two or three years, have large numbers of sheep, and wool enough to go a considerable way toward clothing ourselves.

Flax and hemp we should undoubtedly have in abundance. The immense tracts of new rich land, which may be planted with these articles, would yield immense quantities of them. What large supplies of seed do we annually export to Ireland! When we come to withhold these, and make the cultivation of flax and hemp a matter of serious attention, we shall soon procure a plenty of them. In speaking of this matter, you confine your views to the single small province of New York. You say: "We sow already as much flax as we can conveniently manage. Besides, it requires a rich, free soil; nor will the same ground in *this* country produce flax a second time till after an interval of five or six years. If the measures of the Congress should be carried into full effect, I confess we may, in a year or two, want a large quantity of hemp for the executioner.

26. I may be thought here to contradict my former assertion, to wit, that in eighteen months all the goods we have among us will be consumed; but I only meant that all the goods in the hands of the merchants would be purchased and taken off.

But I fear we must import it. It exhausts the soil too much to be cultivated in the old settled parts of the province."

There is land enough in the other provinces, that is rich, free, and new; nor is it at all liable to the objections you make. As to this particular province, and any others in the same circumstances, let only such parts as are fit be planted with the articles in question, and let the rest be managed as before. Much more may be produced in this than has been hitherto; but if it could not afford a sufficiency for itself, let it exchange its grain with other colonies that superabound with such materials.

If we sow already as much flax as we can conveniently manage, it is because the chief of our attention is engrossed by other things; but the supposition is, that there will be less demand for them, and more for flax; and, by attending less to present objects, we shall have it in our power for the future to sow and manage much more flax than in the time past.

With respect to cotton, you do not pretend to deny that a sufficient quantity of that might be produced. Several of the Southern colonies are so favorable to it that, with due cultivation, in a couple of years they would afford enough to clothe the whole continent.

As to the expense of bringing it by land, the best way will be to manufacture it where it grows, and afterward transport it to the other colonies. Upon this plan I apprehend the expense would not be greater than to build and equip large ships to import the manufactures of Great Britain from thence.

The difficulty of transportation would be attended with one great advantage. It would give employment and bread to a number of people; and would, among other things, serve to prevent there being those terrific bands of thieves, robbers, and highwaymen, which you endeavor to draw up in such formidable array against the Congress.

It would, however, be hardly possible to block up our ports in such a manner as to cut off all communication between the colonies by water.

There would remain some avenues in spite of all that could be done; and we should not be idle in making proper use of them.

I mentioned before the vast quantities of skins in America, which would never let us want a warm and comfortable suit. This is one of our principal resources; and this you have passed over in silence. A suit made of skins would not be quite so elegant as one of broadcloth; but it would shelter us from the inclemency of the winter full as well.

Upon the whole, considering all the resources we have, and the time we shall have to prepare them before we are in actual want, there can be no room to doubt that we may live without the manufactures of Great Britain, if we are careful, frugal, and industrious.

But it is said we have no persons to manufacture our materials after we have provided them. Among the swarms of emigrants that have within these few years past come to the continent, there are numbers of manufacturers in the necessary branches. These, for want of encouragement in their own occupations, have been obliged to apply themselves to other methods of getting a living, but would be glad of an opportunity to return to them. Besides these we should soon have a plenty of workmen from Great Britain and Ireland. Numbers who would be thrown out of employ *there*, would be glad to flock to us for subsistence. They would not stay at home and be miserable while there was any prospect of encouragement here. Neither is there any great difficulty in acquiring a competent knowledge of the manufacturing arts. In a couple of years many of our own people might become proficient enough to make the coarser kinds of stuffs and linens.

But, if it should be necessary, we have other resources besides all these. It will be impossible for the ships of Great Britain to line the vast extended coast of this continent in such a manner as to preclude the admission of foreign aids and supplies. After every possible precaution against it, we shall still be able to get large quantities of goods from France and Holland.[27]

---

27. You may perhaps tell me here, that I contradict the sentiments I formerly delivered, respecting unlawful trade. But it is by no means the case. I despise the practice of ava-

I shall conclude this head with one more observation, which is this: That all such as may be deprived of business by the operation of our measures in America may be employed in cultivating lands. We have enough and to spare. It is of no force to object, that "when our exports are stopped our grain would become of little worth." They can be occupied in raising other things that will be more wanted, to wit, materials for manufactures; and only a sufficiency of provisions for their own use. In such a country as this, there can be no great difficulty in finding business for all its inhabitants. Those obstacles which, to the eye of timidity or disaffection seem like the *Alps*, would, to the hand of resolution and perseverance become mere *hillocks*.

Once more I insist upon it, that Great Britain can never force us to submission by blocking up our ports, and that the consequences of such a procedure to herself, Ireland, and the West Indies, would be too fatal to admit of it. If she is determined to enslave us, it must be by force of arms; and to attempt this, I again assert, would be nothing less than *the grossest infatuation, madness itself.*

Whatever may be said of the disciplined troops of Great Britain, the event of the contest must be extremely doubtful. There is a certain enthusiasm in liberty, that makes human nature rise above itself in acts of bravery and heroism. It cannot be expected that America would yield, without a magnanimous, persevering, and bloody struggle. The testimony of past ages, and the least knowledge of mankind, must suffice to convince us of the contrary. We have a recent instance, in *Corsica*, to what lengths a people will go in defence of its liberties; and if we take a view of the colonies in general, we must perceive that the pulse of Americans beats high in their country's cause. Let us, then, suppose the arms of Great Britain triumphant, and America mutilated, exhausted, and vanquished. What situation will Great Britain then be in? What laurels will she reap from her conquests? Alas, none! Every true friend to that

---

ricious smugglers very heartily; but when a whole people are invaded, there can be no law of any force against their procuring every needful succor.

deluded country must shudder at the prospect of her self-destroying success. The condition we should be left in would disable us from paying the six millions sterling, which is due for the manufactures of Great Britain. Instead of the present millions derived annually from our trade, we should be so distressed and reduced as to be, for many years to come, a burthen, and not an advantage. Millions are soon dispensed in supporting fleets and armies. Much British treasure and blood would be expended in effecting our ruin.

This, then, would be the situation of Great Britain. Her public debt would be augmented several millions. Her merchants, who are one of the principal sources of her opulence, would, many of them, become bankrupt by the loss of the vast sums due them in America. Her manufactures would stagnate and decay, and her revenues would be considerably diminished. This continent, which is now a rich source of wealth and strength, would be debilitated and depressed.

Would the ancient rivals and enemies of Great Britain be idle at such a conjuncture as this? Would they not eagerly seize the opportunity to recover their former losses, and revenge the evils they have sustained on former occasions? It will be said: This is possible, but it may not happen. I answer: Causes must fail of their usual effects if it does not. Princes and nations must cease to be ambitious and avaricious. The French, from being a jealous, politic, and enterprising people, must be grown negligent, stupid, and inattentive to their own interest. They never could have a fairer opportunity, or a greater temptation, to aggrandize themselves and triumph over Great Britain, than would be here presented. Let us imagine England immersed in a war with France, Spain, or any other potent neighbor; with her public debt increased, some of her best springs dried up, and America ruined—not only unable to afford her any assistance, but, perhaps, fired with resentment and a sense of accumulated injuries, ready to throw itself into the arms of her enemies. In these circumstances, what would be the fate of this unhappy kingdom? Every man of discernment must be convinced that ruin would be unavoidable.

But what reason have we to believe the arms of Great Britain would prevail? It will be replied: Because she can send against us some of the best troops in the world, either with respect to valor or discipline; and because we have only a raw, unexperienced militia to oppose them. Discipline and military skill are certainly matters of great importance, and give those to whom they belong a vast superiority; but they do not render them invincible. Superior numbers, joined to natural intrepidity and that animation which is inspired by a desire of freedom and a love of one's country, may very well overbalance those advantages.

I imagine it will be readily allowed that Great Britain could not spare an army of above fifteen thousand men to send against the colonies. These would have to subdue near six hundred thousand. The established rule of computing the number of men capable of bearing arms in any nation, is by taking a fifth part of the whole people. By the best calculations, we are supposed, in America, to exceed three millions. The fifth part of three millions is six hundred thousand. But in order to be certain of our computations, let us suppose there are only five hundred thousand fighting men in the colonies. Then there will be upward of thirty Americans to one British soldier. A great disparity indeed! And such as never can be compensated by any discipline or skill whatever! It will be objected that these five hundred thousand cannot act together. I grant it; nor is there any occasion that they should. Forty thousand will be a sufficient number to make head at a time; and these must be kept up by fresh supplies as fast as there is any diminution.

Let it be remembered that there are no large plains for the two armies to meet in and decide the contest by some decisive stroke; where any advantage gained by either side might be prosecuted till a complete victory was obtained. The circumstances of our country put it in our power to evade a pitched battle. It will be better policy to harass and exhaust the soldiery by frequent skirmishes and incursions than to take the open field with them, by which means they would have the full benefit of their superior regularity and skill. Americans are better qualified for that kind of fighting, which is most adapted to this country, than regular troops. Should the soldiery advance into the country, as they would be obliged

to do if they had any inclination to subdue us, their discipline would be
of little use to them. We should, in that case, be at least upon an equality
with them, in any respect; and as we should have the advantage on many
accounts, they would be likely to gain nothing by their attempts.

Several of the colonies are now making preparation for the worst (and
indeed the best way to avoid a civil war is to be prepared for it). They
are disciplining men as fast as possible, and in a few months will be able
to produce many thousands not so much inferior in the essentials of
discipline as may perhaps be imagined. A little actual service will put
them very nearly upon a footing with their enemies. The history of the
Swedes and Russians, under Charles XII. and Peter the Great, will teach
us how soon a people, possessed of natural bravery, may be brought to
equal the most regular troops. The Swedes at first obtained very signal
advantages, but after a while the Russians learned to defeat them with
equal numbers. It is true there was one of the greatest men the world
has seen at the head of the latter; but there was one who emulated the
Macedonian conqueror at the head of the former. Charles was, perhaps,
never surpassed by any man in courage or skill; and his soldiers were well
worthy of such a general. There is also this important circumstance in
our favor, when compared with the Russians. They were barbarous and
untractable. We are civilized and docile. They were ignorant even of the
theory of war. We are well acquainted with it, and therefore should more
easily be brought to the practice of it, and be sooner taught that order
and method which we are deficient in.

It is sometimes urged that we have no experienced officers to command us. We labor under some disadvantage in this respect, but not so
great as is believed. There are many who have served in the last war with
reputation, dispersed throughout the colonies. These might have the superior direction of matters; and there are men enough of known sense
and courage who would soon make excellent officers. During the disputes
between the unfortunate *Charles* and the Parliament, many country gentlemen served in the armies of the latter, and signalized themselves for
their military virtues. It is worthy of observation that the present state

of the army is not the most favorable. As is always the consequence of a long peace, there are many effeminate striplings among the officers, who are better calculated to marshal the forces of *Venus* than to conduct the sturdy sons of *Mars*. There are, comparatively, but few veterans, either among the leaders or the common soldiers.

You ask me: What resources have the colonies to pay, clothe, arm, and feed their troops? I refer you to the accounts of Virginia and Marblehead for an answer to this question. Our troops, on the spot with us, will be much more easily maintained than those of Great Britain at such a distance. We are not so poor and encumbered as to be unable to support those who are immediately employed in defending our liberties. Our country abounds in provisions. We have already materials enough among us, to keep us in clothes longer than Great Britain would have any appetite to continue her hostilities. Several of the colonies are pretty well stored with ammunition. France, Spain, and Holland would find means to supply us with whatever we wanted.[28]

Let it not be said that this last is a bare *possibility;* that France and Spain have promised not to interfere in the dispute; and that Holland has long been a faithful ally to the British nation. There is the highest degree of probability in the case. A more desirable object to France and Spain than the disunion of these colonies from Great Britain cannot be imagined. Every dictate of policy and interest would prompt them to forward it by every possible means. They could not take any so effectual method to destroy the growing power of their great rival. The promises of princes and statesmen are of little weight. They never bind longer than till a strong temptation offers to break them; and they are frequently made with a sinister design. If we consult the known character of the French, we shall be disposed to conclude that their present seemingly pacific and friendly disposition is merely a piece of *finesse,* intended to

28. This is certainly a very remarkable prediction for a boy of eighteen, and shows as well as anything the penetrating mind which Talleyrand appreciated when he said of Hamilton, "Il a diviné l'Europe."

dupe the administration into some violent measures with the colonies, that they may improve them to their own advantage. The most that can be expected is, that they would refrain from any open rupture with Great Britain. They would undoubtedly take every clandestine method to introduce among us supplies of those things which we stood in need of to carry on the dispute. They would not neglect any thing in their power to make the opposition on our part as vigorous and obstinate as our affairs would admit of.

With respect to Holland, notwithstanding express engagements to the contrary, her merchants, during the last war, were constantly supplying the French and Spaniards with military stores and other things they had occasion for. The same, or perhaps more powerful, motives would influence them to assist us in a like manner.

But it seems to me a mark of great credulity to believe, upon the strength of their assurance, that France and Spain would not take a still more interesting part in the affair. The disjunction of these colonies from Great Britain, and the acquisition of a free trade with them, are objects of too inviting a complexion to suffer those kingdoms to remain idle spectators of the contention. If they found us inclined to throw ourselves upon their protection, they would eagerly embrace the opportunity to weaken their antagonist and strengthen themselves. Superadded to these general and prevailing inducements, there are others of a more particular nature. They would feel no small inconvenience in the loss of those supplies they annually get from us; and their islands in the West Indies would be in the greatest distress for want of our trade.

From these reflections it is more than probable that America is able to support its freedom, even by the force of arms, if she be not betrayed by her own sons. And in whatever light we view the matter, the consequences to Great Britain would be too destructive to permit her to proceed to extremities, unless she has lost all just sense of her own interest.

You say: "The grand Congress, the *piddling* committees, through the continent, have *all* disclaimed their subjection to the sovereign authority of the empire. They deny the authority of Parliament to make any laws to bind them at all. They claim an absolute independency. Great Britain has no choice but to declare the colonies independent states, or to try the force of arms in order to bring them to a sense of their duty."

It is the common trick of ministerial writers, to represent the Congress as having made some new demands, which were unknown to former times; whereas, in truth, they have, in substance, acknowledged the only dependence on Parliament which was ever intended by their predecessors. Nor is it true, that they have claimed an *absolute independency*. It is insulting common-sense to say so, when it is notorious that they have acknowledged the right of Parliament to regulate the trade of the colonies. Any further dependence on it is unnecessary and dangerous. They have professed allegiance to the British king, and have bound themselves, on any emergency, to contribute their proportion of men and money, to the defence and protection of the whole empire. Can this be called *absolute independency?* Is it better for Great Britain to hazard the total loss of these colonies, than to hold them upon these conditions? Is it preferable to make enemies of the people of America, instead of being connected with them by the equal tie of fellow-subjects? Is it not madness to run the risk of losing the trade of these colonies, from which the mother country drew[29] "more clear profit than Spain has drawn from all her mines," because they insist only upon all the essential rights of freemen? You may call it effrontery, consummate assurance, or what you please, to say so; but every man, capable of taking a full prospect of all the probable mischiefs which may result from an open rupture between Great Britain and the colonies, will coincide with me when I affirm that nothing but the most *frantic extravagance* can influence the administration to attempt the reduction of America by force of arms.

It is sufficiently evident, from the respective charters, that the rights we now claim are coeval with the original settlement of these colonies.

---

29. See Shipley's speech. [The quotation that follows is from Jonathan Shipley, *A Speech Intended to Have Been Spoken on the Bill for Altering the Charters of the Colony of Massachusett's Bay* (London, 1774).]

These rights have been, at different times, strenuously asserted, though they have been suffered to be violated in several instances, through inattention, or, perhaps, an unwillingness to quarrel with the mother country. I shall decline producing any other proofs of the sense of the other provinces than those already mentioned, and shall confine myself to a few extracts from the resolves of some assemblies of this province.

In 1691, there was an act passed by the General Assembly, which contained the following clauses.[30]

"Be it enacted, by the Governor, Council, and Representatives, met in General Assembly, and it is hereby enacted and declared by the authority of the same, that the *supreme legislative power and authority,* under their Majesties, William and Mary, King and Queen of England, etc., shall for ever be, and reside, in a Governor-in-Chief and Council, appointed by their Majesties, their heirs and successors, and the people by their representatives met and convened in General Assembly.

"That no freeman shall be taken or imprisoned, or be deprived of his freehold, or life, or liberty, or free customs, or outlawed, or exiled, or any otherways destroyed; nor shall be passed upon, adjudged, or condemned, but *by the lawful judgment of his peers, and by the law of the province.*

"That no *aid, tax, tallage, custom, loan, benevolence, gift, excise, duty,* or *imposition whatsoever,* shall be laid, assessed, imposed, levied, or required of, or on, any of their Majesties' subjects within this province, etc., or their estates, *upon any manner of color or pretence whatsoever,* but by the act and consent of the Governor and Council, and Representatives of the people, in General Assembly met and convened."

This act shows clearly the sense of his Majesty's representative, his Council, and the Assembly of this province, above *eighty years* ago, which was, that the supreme legislative authority, and the exclusive power of taxation, should for ever be, and reside, in a Governor-in-Chief and

---

30. This act is very remarkable. It was drawn up by Messrs. *Tazewell* and *Emmett,* two gentlemen appointed by the governor for the purpose, and remained *six years* in England before there was a negative put upon it.

Council appointed by their Majesties, their heirs and successors; and the people, by their representatives met and convened in General Assembly.

We may also infer from hence, that the other colonies actually enjoyed similar privileges at that time; for it would have been the height of presumption, in this province, to claim such important immunities, had not the others been in possession of the like.

This act, of itself, confutes all that has been said concerning the novelty of our present claims; and proves, that the injurious reflections on the Congress, for having risen in their demands, are malicious and repugnant to truth.

You have produced some expressions of the Congress and Assembly of this province, in 1765, which you lay great stress upon. The true meaning of them may be gathered from the following passage, which is taken from the same piece that contains the expressions in question. The Congress speak thus: "It is humbly submitted, whether there be not a material distinction, in reason and sound policy at least, between the necessary exercise of parliamentary jurisdiction in general Acts for the amendment of the common law and the regulation of trade and commerce through the whole empire, and the exercise of that jurisdiction by imposing taxes on the colonies."

They allow only a power of making *general acts* for the amendment of the *common law* and for the general regulation of trade. As to any special laws to bind the colonies, in particular, they never intended submission to these; nor could they intend a right to impose special duties of any kind for the purpose of raising a revenue, which is to all intents and purposes a species of taxation.

The resolves of our Assembly, the last day of December, 1771, about three years afterward, will serve as a full explanation.

"As it is not only the common birthright of all his Majesty's subjects, but is also essential to the preservation of the peace, strength, and prosperity of the British empire, that an *exact equality of constitutional rights* among all his Majesty's subjects in the several parts of the empire be uniformly and invariably maintained and supported; and as it would be inconsistent with the constitutional rights of his Majesty's subjects in Great Britain to tax them, either in person or estate, without the consent of their representatives in Parliament assembled: It is therefore

"RESOLVED, *nemine contradicente:*

"That it is the opinion of this Committee, that *no tax under any name, or denomination, or on any pretence, or for any purpose whatsoever,* can or ought to be imposed, or levied, upon the persons, estates, or property of his Majesty's good subjects within this colony, *but of their free gift, by their representatives lawfully convened in General Assembly.*

"That it is the opinion of this Committee, that this colony lawfully and constitutionally has, and enjoys, an internal legislature, in which the Crown and the people of this colony are constitutionally represented; and that *the power and authority of the said legislature cannot lawfully or constitutionally be suspended, abridged, abrogated, or annulled, by any power or prerogative whatsoever;* the prerogative of the crown, ordinarily exercised for prorogations and dissolutions, only excepted."

A supreme authority in the Parliament to make any special laws for this province, consistent with the internal legislature here claimed, is impossible and cannot be supposed, without falling into that solecism in politics, of *imperium in imperio.*

I imagine sir, I have, by this time pretty fully and satisfactorily answered every thing contained in your letter of any consequence. The parts I have left unattended to are such as cannot operate, materially, to the prejudice of the cause I espouse; but I should not have neglected them, had it not been that I have already taken a very ample range, and it would perhaps be imprudent to delay a conclusion.

Whatever opinion may be entertained of my sentiments and intentions, I attest that Being, whose all-seeing eye penetrates the inmost recesses of the heart, that I am not influenced (in the part I take) by any unworthy motive; that, if I am in an error, it is my judgment, not my heart, that errs; that I earnestly lament the unnatural quarrel between the parent state and the colonies, and most ardently wish for a speedy reconciliation—a perpetual and *mutually* beneficial union; that I am a warm advocate for limited monarchy, and an unfeigned well-wisher to the present Royal Family.

But, on the other hand, I am inviolably attached to the essential rights of mankind and the true interests of society. I consider civil liberty, in a genuine, unadulterated sense, as the greatest of terrestrial blessings. I am convinced that the whole human race is entitled to it, and that it can be wrested from no part of them without the blackest and most aggravated guilt.

I verily believe, also, that the best way to secure a permanent and happy union between Great Britain and the colonies, is to permit the latter to be as free as they desire. To abridge their liberties, or to exercise any power over them which they are unwilling to submit to, would be a perpetual source of discontent and animosity. A continual jealousy would exist on both sides. This would lead to tyranny on the one hand, and to sedition and rebellion on the other. Impositions, not really grievous in themselves, would be thought so, and the murmurs arising from thence would be considered as the effect of a turbulent, ungovernable spirit. These jarring principles would at length throw all things into disorder, and be productive of an irreparable breach and a total disunion.

That harmony and mutual confidence may speedily be restored between all the parts of the British empire, is the favorite wish of one who feels the warmest sentiments of good-will to mankind, who bears no enmity to you, and who is

A SINCERE FRIEND TO AMERICA.

REMARKS ON THE QUEBEC BILL

The same parliamentary session that passed the Coercive Acts in 1774 also passed new legislation for the governance of predominantly Catholic Francophone Quebec, which had been won from France in the Seven Years' War. Ostensibly a measure to grant "the free exercise of the religion of the Church of Rome" to a colony of officially Protestant Britain, the Quebec Act deeply unnerved the thirteen colonies. In the first place, the act recognized "accustomed dues and rights" of Catholic clergy as part of "toleration," which amounted to royal sanction for mandatory tithing to the Catholic Church. In the second place, the act dramatically increased the boundaries of the province of Quebec, pushing them far south into what are today the states of Ohio, Michigan, Indiana, Illinois, and Wisconsin. Since the western land claims of the colonies seemed implied by their charters, the colonists of Massachusetts, New York, Connecticut, and Virginia saw the act as a gigantic swindle. Third, as New France, Quebec had been ruled directly by an agent of the French king, an intendant, and had never enjoyed representation in colonial government; the Quebec Act restored this *status quo antebellum* politically by making Quebec a royally administered colony. Finally, there was more than a century's association in the British Whig tradition of Catholicism with absolutism, an association, for example, made by John Locke, who, during the dangerous reign of James II, disguised his folio manuscript of *Two Treatises of Government* with the title "On the French Disease."

During the Glorious Revolution against the absolutist ambitions of James II, himself a Catholic, the revolutionary slogan was "No Popery! No Slavery!" Colonial fears that the crown was deliberately creating an absolutist Catholic enclave on their flank were not assuaged when, in the course of debating the act, one MP opined, "The Quebec constitution is the only proper constitution for colonies; it ought to have been given to them all, when first planted; and it is what all now ought to be reduced to."[*]

Hamilton's *Remarks on the Quebec Bill* appeared in the columns of James Rivington's *New York Gazeteer* in June 1775.

---

[*] Quoted in George Bancroft, *History of the United States of America* (Cambridge, Mass., 1876), 4:308.

REMARKS ON THE QUEBEC BILL[1]

1775

NO. I

IN COMPLIANCE with my promise to the public, and in order to rescue truth from the specious disguise with which it has been clothed, I shall now offer a few remarks on the act entitled "An act for making more effectual provision for the government of the province of Quebec in North America"; whereby I trust it will clearly appear that arbitrary power and its great engine, the Popish religion, are, to all intents and purposes, established in that province.

While Canada was under the dominion of France, the French laws and customs were in force there, which are regulated in conformity to the genius and complexion of a despotic constitution, and expose the lives and properties of subjects to continual depredation from the malice and avarice of those in authority. But when it fell under the dominion of Great Britain, these laws, so unfriendly to the happiness of society, gave place, of course, to the milder influence of the English laws, and his Majesty, by proclamation, promised to all those who should settle there a full enjoyment of the rights of British subjects. In violation of this promise, the act before us declares: "That the said proclamation and the commission under the authority whereof the government of the said province is at present administered, be, and the same are, hereby revoked, annulled, and made void, from and after the first day of May, one thousand seven hundred and seventy-five." This abolition of the privileges stipulated by the proclamation was not inflicted as a penalty for any crime by which a forfeiture had been incurred, but merely on pretence of the

---

1. An Act to Regulate the Government of Quebec. Passed by Parliament in 1774.

present form of government having been found by experience to be in-applicable to the state and circumstances of the province.

I have never heard any satisfactory account concerning the foundation of this pretence, for it does not appear that the people of Canada, at large, ever expressed a discontent with their new establishment, or solic-ited a restoration of their old. They were, doubtless, the most proper judges of the matter, and ought to have been fully consulted before the alteration was made. If we may credit the general current of intelligence which we have had respecting the disposition of the Canadians, we must conclude they are averse to the present regulation of the Parliament, and had rather continue under the form of government instituted by the Royal proclamation.

However this be, the French laws are again revived. It is enacted: "That in all matters of controversy relative to property and civil rights, resort shall be had to the laws of Canada, as the rule for the decision of the same; and all causes that hereafter shall be instituted in any of the courts of justice, shall, with respect to such property and rights, be determined agreeably to the said laws and customs of Canada, until they shall be varied and altered by any ordinances that shall, from time to time, be passed in the said province, by the Governor, Lieutenant-Governor, or Commander-in-Chief for the time being, by and with the advice and consent of the Legislative Council of the same." Thus the ancient laws of Canada are restored, liable to such variations and additions as shall be deemed necessary by the Governor and Council; and as both the one and the other are to be appointed by the king during pleasure, they will be all his creatures, and entirely subject to his will, which is thereby rendered the original fountain of law; and the property and civil rights of the Canadians are made altogether dependent upon it, because the power communicated, of varying and altering, by new ordinances, is in-definite and unlimited. If this does not make the king absolute in Canada, I am at a loss for any tolerable idea of absolute authority, which I have ever thought to consist, with respect to a monarch, in the power of governing his people according to the dictates of his own will. In the present case, he has only to inform the Governor and Council what new laws he would choose to have passed, and their situation will insure their compliance.

It is further provided: "That nothing contained in the act, shall extend, or be construed to extend, to prevent or hinder his Majesty, his heirs and successors, from erecting, constituting, and appointing, from time to time, such courts of criminal, civil, and ecclesiastical jurisdiction, within and for the said province of Quebec, and appointing, from time to time, the judges and officers thereof, as his Majesty, his heirs and successors, shall think necessary for the circumstances of the said province."

Here a power of a most extraordinary and dangerous nature is conferred. There must be an end of all liberty where the prince is possessed of such an exorbitant prerogative as enables him, at pleasure, to establish the most iniquitous, cruel, and oppressive courts of criminal, civil, and ecclesiastical jurisdiction; and to appoint temporary judges and officers, whom he can displace and change as often as he pleases. For what can more nearly concern the safety and happiness of subjects, than the wise economy, and equitable constitution of those courts in which trials for life, liberty, property, and religion are to be conducted? Should it ever comport with the designs of an ambitious and wicked minister, we may see an Inquisition erected in Canada, and priestly tyranny hereafter find as propitious a soil in America as it ever has in Spain or Portugal.

But in order to varnish over the arbitrary complexion of the act, and to conciliate the minds of the Canadians, it is provided: "That whereas, the certainty and lenity of the criminal law of England, and the benefits and advantages resulting from the use of it, have been sensibly felt by the inhabitants, from an experience of more than nine years; Therefore, the same shall be administered and shall be observed as law, in the province of Quebec, to the exclusion of every rule of criminal law which did, or might, prevail in said province before the year one thousand seven hundred and sixty-four."

As "it is in the goodness of criminal laws that the liberty of the subject principally depends,"[2] this would have been an important privilege, had it not been rendered uncertain and alienable by the latter part of the same clause, which makes them "subject to such alterations and amendments as the Governor, Lieutenant Governor, and Commander-in-Chief for the time being, by and with the advice and consent of the Legislative Council of the same, shall, from time to time, cause to be made therein."

Under the notion of necessary alterations and amendments, the king, through the medium of his creatures, the Governor and Council, may entirely new mould the criminal laws of Canada, and make them subservient to the most tyrannical views. So that, in this respect, also, the principle of arbitrary power, which is the soul of the act, is uniformly maintained and preserved, in full vigor, without the least real or effectual diminution.

It has been denied, with the most palpable absurdity, that the right of trial by juries is taken from the Canadians. It is said that the provincial legislature of Canada may introduce them as soon as they please, and it is expected that they will, "as soon as the inhabitants desire them," or "the state of the country will admit of them."

A civil right is that which the laws and the constitution have actually conferred, not that which may be derived from the future bounty and beneficence of those in authority. The possibility that the Legislature of Canada may hereafter introduce trials by juries, does not imply a right in the people to enjoy them. For in the same sense it may be said that the inhabitants of France, or Spain, have a right to trial by juries, because it is equally in the power of their Legislatures to establish them.

Since, therefore, it is apparent that a system of French laws has been established in the province of Quebec, and an indefinite power vested in the king, to vary and alter these laws, as also to constitute such courts of criminal, civil, and ecclesiastical jurisdiction and to introduce such a form

2. Montesquieu. [The quotation is from Montesquieu, *The Spirit of the Laws* (Cambridge, 1989), 188.]

of criminal law as he shall judge necessary; I say, since all this is deducible from the express letter of the act, or, in other words, since the whole legislative, executive, and judiciary powers are ultimately and effectually, though not immediately, lodged in the king, there can be no room to doubt that an arbitrary government has been really instituted throughout the extensive region now comprised in the province of Quebec.

NO. II

Having considered the nature of this bill with regard to civil government, I am next to examine it with relation to religion, and to endeavor to show that the Church of Rome has now the sanction of a legal establishment in the province of Quebec.

In order to do this the more satisfactorily I beg leave to adopt the definition given of an established religion by a certain writer who has taken great pains to evince the contrary. "An established religion," says he, "is a religion which the civil authority engages not only to protect but to support." This act makes effectual provision not only for the protection but for the permanent support of Popery, as is evident from the following clause: "And for the more perfect security and ease of the minds of the inhabitants of the said province, it is hereby declared that his Majesty's subjects, professing the religion of the Church of Rome, in the said province, may have, hold, and enjoy the free exercise of the religion of the Church of Rome, subject to the king's supremacy, etc., and that the clergy of the said Church may hold, receive, and enjoy their accustomed dues and rights," etc.

This is represented as a bare permission to the clergy to enjoy the usual emoluments of their functions, and not as a legal provision for their support. Much stress seems to be laid on the word "*may*," which is commonly italicized. But though the phraseology be artful, yet it is easy to perceive that it operates to the same effect as if it had been more positive and emphatical.

The clergy "may hold, receive, and enjoy their accustomed dues and rights." They may if they please. It is at their option, and must depend upon their will; and, consequently, there must be a correspondent obligation upon their parishioners to comply with that will, and to pay those dues when required. What the law gives us an unconditional permission to enjoy, no person can legally withhold from us. It becomes our property, and we can enforce our right to it. If the Legislature of this colony were to decree that the clergy of the different denominations may hold, receive, and enjoy tithes of their respective congregations, we should soon find that it would have the same efficacy as if it were decreed that the several congregations should pay tithes to their respective clergy. For, otherwise, the Legislature might confer a right which had no correlative obligation, and which must, therefore, be void and inefficacious. But this is contradictory and impossible.

"Tithes in Canada," it is said, "are the property of the Roman Church; and permitting a tolerated church to enjoy its own property, is far short of the idea of an establishment." But I should be glad to know, in the first place, how tithes can be the property of any but of an established church? And in the next, how they came to be the property of the Romish Church in Canada, during the intermediate space between the surrender of that province to the English and the passing of this act? Nothing can be deemed my property, to which I have not a perfect and uncontrollable right by the laws. If a church have not a similar right to tithes, it can have no property in them; and if it have, it is plain the laws must have made provision for its support, or, in other words, must have established it.

Previous to the surrender of Canada the Catholic religion was established there by the laws of France; and tithes were, on that account, the legal property of the Church of Rome, and could not be withheld by the laity though ever so much disposed to it. But after the surrender this circumstance took a different turn. The French laws being no longer in force, the establishment of the Romish Church ceased of course, and with it the property which it before had in tithes.

It is true the clergy may have continued to receive and enjoy their customary dues, tithes, and other perquisites; but they were not for all that the property of the church, because it had lost its legal right to them, and it was at the discretion of the laity to withhold them, if they had thought proper, or to abridge them, and place them upon a more moderate footing. Their voluntary concurrence was necessary to give their priests a right to demand them as before. But by the late act this matter is again put into its former situation. Tithes are now become the *property* of the church as formerly, because it again has a legal claim to them, and the conditional consent of the people is set aside. Thus we see that this act does not, in fact, permit a tolerated church to enjoy "its own property," but gives it a real and legal property in that which it before held from the bounty and liberality of its professors, and which they might withhold or diminish at pleasure; and this, in the most proper sense, converts it into an establishment.

The characteristic difference between a tolerated and established religion consists in this: With respect to the support of the former, the law is passive and improvident, leaving it to those who profess it to make as much, or as little, provision as they shall judge expedient; and to vary and alter that provision, as their circumstances may require. In this manner the Presbyterians and other sects are tolerated in England. They are allowed to exercise their religion without molestation, and to maintain their clergy as they think proper. These are wholly dependent upon their congregations, and can exact no more than they stipulate and are satisfied to contribute. But with respect to the support of the latter, the law is active and provident. Certain precise dues (tithes, etc.) are legally annexed to the clerical office, independent on the liberal contributions of the people; which is exactly the case with the Canadian priests; and, therefore, no reasonable, impartial man will doubt that the religion of the Church of Rome is established in Canada. While tithes were the free, though customary, gift of the people, as was the case before the passing of the act in question, the Roman Church was only in a state of toleration; but when the law came to take cognizance of them, and, by determining their permanent existence, destroyed the free agency of the people, it then resumed the nature of an establishment, which it had been divested of at the time of the capitulation.

As to the Protestant religion, it is often asserted that ample provision has been made by the act for its future establishment; to prove which the writer before mentioned has quoted a clause in the following mutilated manner: "It is provided," says he, "that his Majesty, his heirs or successors, may make such provision out of the accustomed dues, or rights, for the encouragement of the Protestant religion, and for the maintenance of a Protestant clergy within the said province, as he or they shall, from time to time, think necessary and expedient."

It must excite a mixture of anger and disdain to observe the wretched arts to which a designing administration and its abettors are driven in order to conceal the enormity of their measures. This whole clause, in its true and original construction, is destitute of meaning; and was evidently inserted for no other end than to *deceive* by the *appearance* of a provident regard for the Protestant religion. The act first declares: "That his Majesty's subjects professing the religion of the Church of Rome may have and enjoy the free exercise of their religion; and that the clergy of the said church may hold, receive, and enjoy their accustomed dues and rights." Then follows this clause: "Provided, nevertheless, that it shall be lawful for his Majesty, his heirs and successors, to make such provision, out of the rest of the said accustomed dues and rights, for the encouragement of the Protestant religion, for the maintenance and support of a Protestant clergy within the said province, as he or they shall, from time to time, think necessary and expedient."

Thus we see the Romish clergy are to have, hold, and enjoy their accustomed dues and rights, and the *rest* and remainder of them is to be applied toward the encouragement of the Protestant religion; but when they have had their wonted dues, I fancy it will puzzle the administration, by any effort of political chemistry, to produce the *rest*, or remainder. Suppose, for instance, A made an actual settlement of a hundred pounds on B; and, by a subsequent act, should declare that B should continue to hold and enjoy his accustomed and annual bounty; and that the *rest* of the said bounty should be given to C: it is evident that C would have nothing, because there would be no *rest* whatever. Exactly parallel and analogous is the case in hand. The Romish priests are to have their accustomed dues and rights; and the *rest* of the said dues and rights is to be dedicated to the encouragement of the Protestant religion. In the above-recited quotation there is a chasm, the words "the *rest* of" being artfully omitted, to give the passage some meaning which it has not in itself. With this amendment, the sense must be that his Majesty might appropriate what portion of the customary revenues of the Romish clergy he should think proper to the support and maintenance of Protestant churches. But, according to the real words of the act, he can only devote "the rest," or remainder, of such revenues to that purpose, which, as I have already shown, is nothing. So that the seeming provision in favor of the Protestant religion is entirely verbal and delusory. Excellent must be the encouragement it will derive from this source. But this is not all. Had there been really provision made, to be applied at the discretion of his Majesty, I should still consider this act as an atrocious infraction on the rights of Englishmen, in a point of the most delicate and momentous concern. No Protestant Englishman would consent to let the free exercise of his religion depend upon the mere pleasure of any man, however great or exalted. The privilege of worshipping the Deity in the manner his conscience dictates, which is one of the dearest he enjoys, must in that case be rendered insecure and precarious. Yet this is the unhappy situation to which the Protestant inhabitants of Canada are now reduced.

The will of the king must give law to their consciences. It is in his power to keep them for ever dispossessed of all religious immunities, and there is too much reason to apprehend that the same motives which instigated the act would induce him to give them as little future encouragement as possible.

I imagine it will clearly appear, from what has been offered, that the Roman Catholic religion, instead of being tolerated, as stipulated by the treaty of peace, is established by the late act, and that the Protestant religion has been left entirely destitute and unbefriended in Canada. But if there should be any who think that the indulgence granted does not extend to a perfect establishment, and that it may be justified by the terms of the treaty and the subsequent conduct of the Canadians, and if they should also be at a loss to perceive the dangerous nature of the act, with respect to the other colonies, I would beg their further attention to the following considerations.

However justifiable this act may be in relation to the province of Quebec, with its ancient limits, it cannot be defended by the least plausible pretext, when it is considered as annexing such a boundless extent of new territory to the old.

If a free form of government had "been found by experience to be inapplicable to the state and circumstances of the province," and if "a toleration less generous—although it might have fulfilled the letter of the articles of the treaty—would not have answered the expectations of the Canadians, nor have left upon their minds favorable impressions of British justice and honor"—if these reasons be admitted as true, and allowed their greatest weight, they only prove that it might be just and politic to place the province of Quebec, alone, with its former boundaries, in the circumstances of civil and religious government which are established by this act. But when it is demanded, why it has also added the immense tract of country that surrounds all these colonies to that province, and has placed the whole under the same exceptionable institutions, both civil and religious, the advocates for administration must be confounded and silenced.

This act develops the dark designs of the ministry more fully than any thing they have done, and shows that they have formed a systematic project of absolute power.

The present policy of it is evidently this: By giving a legal sanction to the accustomed dues of the priests, it was intended to interest them in behalf of the administration; and by means of the dominion they possessed over the minds of the laity, together with the appearance of good-will toward their religion, to prevent any dissatisfaction which might arise from the loss of their civil rights, and to propitiate them to the great purposes in contemplation—first, the subjugation of the colonies, and afterward that of Great Britain itself. It was necessary to throw out some such lure to reconcile them to the exactions of that power which has been communicated to the king, and which the emergency of the times may require in a very extensive degree.

The future policy of it demands particular attention. The nature of its civil government will hereafter put a stop to emigrations from other parts of the British dominions thither, and from all other free countries. The preeminent advantages secured to the Roman Catholic religion will discourage all Protestant settlers, of whatever nation; and on these accounts, the province will be settled and inhabited by none but Papists. If lenity and moderation are observed in administering the laws, the natural advantages of this fertile infant country, united to the indulgence given to their religion, will attract droves of emigrants from all the Roman Catholic States in Europe, and these colonies, in time, will find themselves encompassed with innumerable hosts of neighbors, disaffected to them, both because of difference in religion and government. How dangerous their situation would be, let every man of common-sense judge.

What can speak in plainer language the corruption of the British Parliament than this act, which invests the king with absolute power over a little world (if I may be allowed the expression), and makes such ample provision for the Popish religion, and leaves the Protestant in such a dependent, disadvantageous situation, that he is like to have no other subjects in this part of his domain, than Roman Catholics, who, by reason of their implicit devotion to their priests, and the superlative reverence they bear those who countenance and favor their religion, will be the voluntary instruments of ambition, and will be ready, at all times, to second the oppressive designs of the administration against the other parts of the empire.

Hence, while our ears are stunned with the dismal sounds of New England's republicanism, bigotry, and intolerance, it behooves us to be upon our guard against the deceitful wiles of those who would persuade us that we have nothing to fear from the operation of the Quebec Act. We should consider it as being replete with danger to ourselves, and as threatening ruin to our posterity. Let us not, therefore, suffer ourselves to be terrified at the prospect of an imaginary and fictitious Scylla; and, by that means, be led blindfold into a real and destructive Charybdis.

PUBLIUS

HAMILTON'S ADOPTION of the *nom de plume* "Publius" reflects his reading while serving as a member of General Washington's staff from 1777 to 1778. He used an Army pay-book as a commonplace book, filled with notes from his wide readings in subjects from finance to history. A particular favorite was Plutarch's *Lives of the Noble Greeks and Romans*, whence he derived the name later associated with *The Federalist Papers*. Publius Valerius was the heroic figure who established republican government in Rome after Lucius Brutus overthrew the tyrant Tarquin the Proud.

These essays were prompted by claims that Samuel Chase (1741–1811), a Maryland member of the Continental Congress, signer of the Declaration of Independence, and later associate justice of the Supreme Court, conspired with a confederate to corner the flour market, with the inside knowledge that the French fleet was due to arrive. My research has turned up no clear evidence of his guilt, but he was dumped from the Maryland congressional delegation, and it seems as though his associates certainly thought him guilty.

The story, however, may be more complicated than appears from Hamilton's tract. Because the Congress lacked tax powers, and because requisitions on the states were unevenly complied with, Congress began issuing paper money to pay its expenses in June 1775. What began with a two-million-dollar issue had, by 1778, become a torrent of paper, one million dollars a week. As inflation began to gallop, Congress searched desperately for expedients to preserve the value of its notes, and the press was filled with stories of peculation and lack of patriotism by war profiteers. One might, in other words, suspect that to some degree it was more convenient to scapegoat the speculators and engrossers who were responsible for rising prices than to lay the blame on the only resource the government had.

Hamilton's essays appeared in the *New York Journal, and the General Advertiser,* October 1778.

PUBLIUS

POUGHKEEPSIE, October 19, 1778.

MR. HOLT:

There are abuses in the state which demand an immediate remedy. Important political characters must be brought upon the stage, and animadverted upon with freedom. The opinion I have of the independence of your spirit convinces me you will ever be a faithful guardian of the liberty of the press, and determines me to commit to you the publication of a series of letters, which will give you an opportunity of exemplifying it.

The following is by way of prelude. You may depend I shall always preserve the decency and respect due either to the Government of the United States, or to the government of any particular State; but I shall not conceive myself bound to use any extraordinary ceremony with the characters of corrupt individuals, however exalted their stations.

To the Printer of the New York "Journal."

SIR:—While every method is taken to bring to justice those men whose principles and practices have been hostile to the present revolution, it is to be lamented that the conduct of another class, equally criminal, and, if possible, more mischievous, has hitherto passed with impunity, and almost without notice. I mean that tribe who, taking advantage of the times, have carried the spirit of monopoly and extortion to an excess which scarcely admits of a parallel. Emboldened by the success of progressive impositions, it has extended to all the necessaries of life. The exorbitant price of every article, and the depreciation upon our currency, are evils derived essentially from this source. When avarice takes the lead in a state, it is commonly the forerunner of its fall. How shocking is it to discover among ourselves, even at this early period, the strongest symptoms of this fatal disease.

There are men in all countries, the business of whose lives it is to raise themselves above indigence by every little art in their power. When these men are observed to be influenced by the spirit I have mentioned, it is nothing more than might be expected, and can only excite contempt. When others, who have characters to support, and credit enough in the world to satisfy a moderate appetite for wealth, in an honorable way, are found to be actuated by the same spirit, our contempt is mixed with indignation. But when a man, appointed to be the guardian of the state and the depositary of the happiness and morals of the people, forgetful of the solemn relation in which he stands, descends to the dishonest artifices of a mercantile projector, and sacrifices his conscience and his trust to pecuniary motives, there is no strain of abhorrence of which the human mind is capable, no punishment the vengeance of the people can inflict, which may not be applied to him with justice.

If it should have happened that a member of Congress has been this degenerate character, and has been known to turn the knowledge of secrets to which his office gave him access to the purposes of private profit, by employing emissaries to engross an article of immediate necessity to the public service, he ought to feel the utmost rigor of public resentment, and be detested as a traitor of the worst and most dangerous kind.

PUBLIUS.

LETTER 2

October 26, 1778.

The Honorable ⸺, Esq.

Sir:—The honor of being a hero of a public panegyric is what you could hardly have aspired to, either from your talents, or from your good qualities. The partiality of your friends has never given you credit for more than mediocrity in the former; and experience has proved that you are indebted for all your consequence to the reverse of the latter. Had you not struck out a new line of prostitution for yourself, you might still have remained unnoticed and contemptible—your name scarcely known beyond the little circle of your electors and clients, and recorded only in the journals of C⸺ss. But you have now forced yourself into view, in a light too singular and conspicuous to be overlooked, and have acquired an undisputed title to be immortalized in infamy. I admire the boldness of your genius, and confess you have exceeded expectation. Though from your first appearance in the world you gave the happiest presages of your future life, and the plainest marks of your being unfettered by any of those nice scruples from which men of principle find so much inconvenience, yet your disposition was not understood in its full extent. You were thought to possess a degree of discretion and natural timidity which would restrain you from any hazardous extremes. You have the merit both of contradicting this opinion, and discovering that, notwithstanding our youth and inexperience as a nation, we begin to emulate the most veteran and accomplished states in the art of corruption. You have shown that America can already boast at least one public character as abandoned as any the history of past or present times can produce.

Were your associates in power of a congenial temper with yourself, you might hope that your address and dexterity upon a late occasion would give a new and advantageous impression of your abilities, and recommend you to employment in some important negotiation, which might afford you other opportunities of gratifying your favorite inclination at the expense of the public.

It is unfortunate for the reputation of Governor Johnston, and for the benevolent purposes of his royal master, that he was not acquainted with the frailties of your character before he made his experiment on men whose integrity was above temptation. If he had known you, and had thought your services worth purchasing, he might have played a sure game, and avoided the risk of exposing himself to contempt and ridicule. And you, sir, might have made your fortune at one decisive stroke.

It is matter of curious inquiry, what could have raised you in the first instance, and supported you since in your present elevation. I never knew a single man but was ready to do ample justice to your demerit. The most indulgent opinion of the qualifications of your head and heart could not offend the modest delicacy of your ear, or give the smallest cause of exultation to your vanity. It is your lot to have the peculiar privilege of being universally despised. Excluded from all resource to your abilities or virtues, there is only one way in which I can account for the rank you hold in the political scale. There are seasons in every country when noise and impudence pass current for worth; and in popular commotions especially, the clamors of interested and factious men are often mistaken for patriotism. You prudently took advantage of the commencement of the contest, to ingratiate yourself in the favor of the people, and gain an ascendant in their confidence by appearing a zealous assertor of their rights. No man will suspect you of the folly of public spirit—a heart notoriously selfish exempts you from any charge of this nature, and obliges us to resolve the part you took into opposite principles. A desire of popularity and a rivalship with the ministry will best explain them. Their attempt to *confine* the sale of a lucrative article of commerce to the East India Company, must have been more unpardonable in the sight of a *monopolist* than the most daring attack upon the public liberty. There is a vulgar maxim which has pointed emphasis in your case, and has made many notable patriots in this dispute.

It sometimes happens that a temporary caprice of the people leads them to make choice of men whom they neither love nor respect; and that they afterward, from an indolent and mechanical habit natural to the human mind, continue their confidence and support merely because they had once conferred them. I cannot persuade myself that your influence rests upon a better foundation, and I think the finishing touch you have given to the profligacy of your character must rouse the recollection of the people, and force them to strip you of a dignity which sets so awkwardly upon you, and consign you to that disgrace which is due to a scandalous perversion of your trust. When you resolved to avail yourself of the extraordinary demand for the article of flour which the wants of the French fleet must produce, and which your official situation early impressed on your attention, to form connections for monopolizing that article, and raising the price upon the public more than one hundred per cent.; when by your intrigues and studied delays you protracted the determination of the C———tt———e of C———ss on the proposals made by Mr. W———sw———th, C———ss———y G———n———l, for procuring the necessary supplies for the public use, to give your agents time to complete their purchases; I say when you were doing all this, and engaging in a traffic infamous in itself, repugnant to your station, and ruinous to your country, did you pause and allow yourself a moment's reflection on the consequences? Were you infatuated enough to imagine you would be able to conceal the part you were acting? Or had you conceived a thorough contempt of reputation, and a total indifference to the opinion of the world? Enveloped in the promised gratifications of your avarice, you probably forgot to consult your understanding, and lost sight of every consideration that ought to have regulated the man, the citizen, the statesman.

I am aware that you could never have done what you have without first obtaining a noble victory over every sentiment of honor and generosity. You have therefore nothing to fear from the reproaches of your own mind. Your insensibility secures you from remorse. But there are arguments powerful enough to extort repentance, even from a temper as callous as yours. You are a man of the world, sir; your self-love forces you to respect its decisions, and your utmost credit with it will not bear the test of your recent enormities, or screen you from the fate you deserve.

LETTER 3

November 16, 1778.

The Honorable ——, Esq.

SIR:—It may appear strange that you should be made a second time the principal figure of a piece intended for the public eye. But a character, insignificant in every other respect, may become interesting from the number and magnitude of its vices. In this view you have a right to the first marks of distinction, and I regret that I feel any reluctance to render you the liberal tribute you deserve. But I reverence humanity, and would not wish to pour a blush upon the cheeks of its advocates. Were I inclined to make a satire upon the species I would attempt a faithful description of your heart. It is hard to conceive, in theory, one of more finished depravity. There are some men whose vices are blended with qualities that cast a lustre upon them, and force us to admire while we detest! Yours are pure and unmixed, without a single solitary excellence even to serve for contrast and variety.

The defects, however, of your private character shall pass untouched. This is a field in which your personal enemies may expatiate with pleasure. I find it enough to consider you in a public capacity.

The station of a member of C——ss is the most illustrious and important of any I am able to conceive. He is to be regarded not only as a legislator, but as a founder of an empire* A man of virtue and ability, dignified with so precious a trust, would rejoice that fortune had given him birth at a time, and placed him in circumstances, so favorable for promoting human happiness. He would esteem it not more the duty than the privilege and ornament of his office to do good to all mankind. From this commanding eminence he would look down with contempt upon every mean or interested pursuit.

To form useful alliances abroad—to establish a wise government at

---

* See Douglas Adair, "Fame and the Founding Fathers," in Trevor Colbourn, ed., *Fame and the Founding Fathers: Essays by Douglas Adair* (Indianapolis, 1974).

home—to improve the internal resources and finances of the nation—would be the generous objects of his care. He would not allow his attention to be diverted from these to intrigue for personal connections to confirm his own influence; nor would he be able to reconcile it, either to the delicacy of his honor or to the dignity of his pride, to confound in the same person the representative of the commonwealth and the little member of a trading company. Anxious for the permanent power and prosperity of the state, he would labor to perpetuate the union and harmony of the several parts. He would not meanly court a temporary importance by patronizing the narrow views of local interest, or by encouraging dissensions either among the people or in C——ss. In council or debate he would discover the candor of a statesman zealous for truth, and the integrity of a patriot studious of the public welfare; not the cavilling petulance of an attorney contending for the triumph of an opinion, nor the perverse duplicity of a partisan devoted to the service of a cabal. Despising the affectation of superior wisdom, he would prove the extent of his capacity by foreseeing evils, and contriving expedients to prevent or remedy them. He would not expose the weak sides of the States to find an opportunity of displaying his own discernment by magnifying the follies and mistakes of others. In his transactions with individuals, whether foreigners or countrymen, his conduct would be guided by the sincerity of a man, and the politeness of a gentleman; not by the temporizing flexibility of a courtier, nor the fawning complaisance of a sycophant.

You will not be at a loss, sir, in what part of this picture to look for your own resemblance; nor have I the least apprehension that you will mistake it on the affirmative side. The happy indifference with which you view those qualities most esteemed for their usefulness to society will preserve you from the possibility of an illusion of this kind. Content with the humble merit of possessing qualities useful only to yourself, you will contemplate your own image on the opposite side with all the satisfaction of conscious deformity.

It frequently happens that the excess of one selfish passion either defeats its own end, or counteracts another. This, if I am not mistaken, is your case. The love of money and the love of power are the predominating ingredients of your mind; cunning, the characteristic of your understanding. This has hitherto carried you successfully through life, and has alone raised you to the exterior consideration you enjoy. The natural consequence of success is temerity. It has now proceeded one step too far, and precipitated you into measures from the consequence of which you will not easily extricate yourself. Your avarice will be fatal to your ambition. I have too good an opinion of the sense and spirit, to say nothing of the virtue, of your countrymen, to believe they will permit you any longer to abuse their confidence or trample upon their honor. Admirably fitted in many respects for the meridian of St. James, you might there make the worthy representative of a venal borough, but you ought not to be suffered to continue to sully the majesty of the people in an American C——ss.

It is a mark of comparison, to which you are not entitled, to advise you by a timely and voluntary retreat to avoid the ignominy of a formal dismission. Your career has held out as long as you could have hoped. It is time you should cease to personate the fictitious character you have assumed, and appear what you really are. Lay aside the mask of patriotism, and assert your station among the honorable tribe of speculators and projectors. Cultivate a close alliance with your —— and your ——, the accomplices and instruments of your guilt, and console yourself for the advantage you have lost, by indulging your genius without restraint in all the forms and varieties of fashionable peculation.

PUBLIUS.

THE CONTINENTALIST

Hamilton resigned from Washington's staff in February 1781 after three years as one of Washington's closest aides. Although he was eager to acquire a battlefield command, while he waited for a new assignment, he continued his reading in political economy and finance. It was during this interlude that he wrote a long letter to Robert Morris, the newly named congressional superintendent of finance, congratulating him on his appointment, and offering his views on the requirements for establishing a sound credit and financial structure for the country.* He ranged over topics from the amount of circulating media required, the tax burden sustainable by the nation, and a detailed plan for the creation of a national bank. Hamilton's proposal for a bank was offered up as a means of making loans from Dutch bankers go further; stretching loans was a key concern, as it was by now the last resource Congress had, paper money issues having finally reached the point where another effort at note issue would simply not be accepted. Despite the ratification of the Articles of Confederation in February 1781, Congress was entirely dependent upon requisitions on the states.

Hamilton's frustration with what he perceived to be the utter worthlessness of Congress had been growing for years, and now, in the after-

* Alexander Hamilton to Robert Morris, April 30, 1781, in Harold Syrett and Jacob E. Cooke, eds., *Papers of Alexander Hamilton* (New York: Columbia University Press, 1961), 2:604–32.

math of his sustained research and writing on one aspect of the problem, he set out to advocate for his signature strong government nationalism in newspaper essays that appeared between July and August 1781 in the *New York Packet.*

THE CONTINENTALIST

Published by Loudon's New York Packet Company

FISHKILL, July 12, 1781.

MR. LOUDON:

I send you the first number of a series of papers which I intend to publish on matters of the greatest importance to these States. I hope they will be read with as much candor and attention as the object of them deserves, and that no conclusions will be drawn till these are fully developed.

 I am, sir,

  Your most ob't humble servant,

        A. B.

NO. I

It would be the extreme of vanity in us not to be sensible that we began this revolution with very vague and confined notions of the practical business of government. To the greater part of us it was a novelty; of those who under the former constitution had had opportunities of acquiring experience, a large proportion adhered to the opposite side, and the remainder can only be supposed to have possessed ideas adapted to the narrow colonial sphere in which they had been accustomed to move, not of that enlarged kind suited to the government of an independent nation.

There were, no doubt, exceptions to these observations—men in all respects qualified for conducting the public affairs with skill and advantage. But their number was small; they were not always brought forward in our councils; and when they were, their influence was too commonly borne down by the prevailing torrent of ignorance and prejudice.

On a retrospect, however, of our transactions, under the disadvantages with which we commenced, it is perhaps more to be wondered at that we have done so well than that we have not done better. There are, indeed, some traits in our conduct as conspicuous for sound policy as others for magnanimity. But, on the other hand, it must also be confessed, there have been many false steps, many chimerical projects and utopian speculations, in the management of our civil as well as of our military affairs. A part of these were the natural effects of the spirit of the times, dictated by our situation. An extreme jealousy of power is the attendant on all popular revolutions, and has seldom been without its evils. It is to this source we are to trace many of the fatal mistakes which have so deeply endangered the common cause; particularly that defect which will be the object of these remarks—a want of power in Congress.

The present Congress, respectable for abilities and integrity, by experience convinced of the necessity of change, are preparing several important articles, to be submitted to the respective States, for augmenting the powers of the Confederation. But though there is hardly at this time a man of information in America who will not acknowledge, as a general proposition, that in its present form it is unequal either to a vigorous prosecution of the war or to the preservation of the Union in peace; yet when the principle comes to be applied to practice, there seems not to be the same agreement in the modes of remedying the defect; and it is to be feared, from a disposition which appeared in some of the States on a late occasion, that the salutary intentions of Congress may meet with more delay and opposition than the critical posture of the States will justify.

It will be attempted to show, in a course of papers, what ought to be done, and the mischiefs of a contrary policy.

In the first stages of the controversy, it was excusable to err. Good intentions, rather than great skill, were to have been expected from us. But we have now had sufficient time for reflection, and experience as ample as unfortunate, to rectify our errors. To persist in them becomes disgraceful, and even criminal, and belies that character of good sense, and a quick discernment of our interests, which, in spite of our mistakes, we have been hitherto allowed. It will prove that our sagacity is limited to interests of inferior moment, and that we are incapable of those enlightened and liberal views necessary to make us a great and a flourishing people.

History is full of examples where, in contests for liberty, a jealousy of power has either defeated the attempts to recover or preserve it, in the first instance, or has afterward subverted it by clogging government with too great precautions for its felicity, or by leaving too wide a door for sedition and popular licentiousness. In a government framed for durable liberty, not less regard must be paid to giving the magistrate a proper degree of authority to make and execute the laws with rigor, than to guard against encroachments upon the rights of the community. As too much power leads to despotism, too little leads to anarchy, and both, eventually, to the ruin of the people. These are maxims well known, but never sufficiently attended to, in adjusting the frames of governments. Some momentary interest or passion is sure to give a wrong bias, and pervert the most favorable opportunities.

No friend to order or to rational liberty can read without pain and disgust the history of the Commonwealths of Greece. Generally speaking, they were a constant scene of the alternate tyranny of one part of the people over the other, or of a few usurping demagogues over the whole. Most of them had been originally governed by kings, whose despotism (the natural disease of monarchy) had obliged their subjects to murder, expel, depose, or reduce them to a nominal existence, and institute popular governments. In these governments, that of Sparta excepted, the jealousy of power hindered the people from trusting out of their own hands a competent authority to maintain the repose and stability of the Commonwealth; whence originated the frequent revolutions and civil broils with which they were distracted. This, and the want of a solid federal union to restrain the ambition and rivalship of the different cities, after a rapid succession of bloody wars, ended in their total loss of liberty, and subjugation to foreign powers.

In comparison of our governments with those of the ancient republics, we must, without hesitation, give the preference to our own; because every power with us is exercised by representation, not in tumultuary assemblies of the collective body of the people, where the art or impudence of the *Orator* or *Tribune,* rather than the utility or justice of the measure, could seldom fail to govern. Yet, whatever may be the advantage on our side in such a comparison, men who estimate the value of institutions, not from prejudices of the moment, but from experience and reason, must be persuaded that the same *jealousy* of *power* has prevented our reaping all the advantages from the examples of other nations which we ought to have done, and has rendered our constitutions in many respects feeble and imperfect.

Perhaps the evil is not very great in respect to our State constitutions; for, notwithstanding their imperfections, they may for some time be made to operate in such a manner as to answer the purposes of the common defence and the maintenance of order; and they seem to have, in themselves, and in the progress of society among us, the seeds of improvement.

But this is not the case with respect to the Federal Government; if it is too weak at first, it will continually grow weaker. The ambition and local interests of the respective members will be constantly undermining and usurping upon its prerogatives till it comes to a dissolution, if a partial combination of some of the more powerful ones does not bring it to a more *speedy* and *violent end.*

NO. II

July 19, 1781.

In a single state where the sovereign power is exercised by delegation, whether it be a limited monarchy or a republic, the danger most commonly is, that the sovereign will become too powerful for his constituents. In federal governments, where different states are represented in a general council, the danger is on the other side—that the members will

be an overmatch for the common head; or, in other words, that it will
not have sufficient influence and authority to secure the obedience of the
several parts of the confederacy.

In a single state the sovereign has the whole legislative power as well
as the command of the national forces—of course an immediate control
over the persons and property of the subjects; every other power is subordinate and dependent. If he undertakes to subvert the constitution, it
can only be preserved by a general insurrection of the people. The mag-
istrates of the provinces, counties, or towns into which the State is divided, having only an executive and police jurisdiction, can take no decisive measures for counteracting the first indications of tyranny; but
must content themselves with the ineffectual weapon of petition and
remonstrance. They cannot raise money, levy troops, nor form alliances.
The leaders of the people must wait till their discontents have ripened
into a general revolt, to put them in a situation to confer the powers
necessary for their defence. It will always be difficult for this to take
place; because the sovereign, possessing the appearance and forms of legal
authority, having the forces and revenues of the state at his command,
and a large party among the people besides—which with those advantages he can hardly fail to acquire—he will too often be able to baffle the
first motions of the discontented, and prevent that union and concert
essential to the success of their opposition.

The security, therefore, of the public liberty must consist in such a
distribution of the sovereign power, as will make it morally impossible
for one part to gain an ascendency over the others, or for the whole to
unite in a scheme of usurpation.

In federal governments, each member has a distinct sovereignty, makes
and executes laws, imposes taxes, distributes justice, and exercises every
other function of government. It has always within itself the means of
revenue; and on an emergency, can levy forces. If the common sovereign
should meditate or attempt any thing unfavorable to the general liberty,
each member, having all the proper organs of power, can prepare for
defence with celerity and vigor. Each can immediately sound the alarm

to the others, and enter into leagues for mutual protection. If the combination is general, as is to be expected, the usurpers will soon find themselves without the means of recruiting their treasury or their armies; and for want of continued supplies of men and money, must, in the end, fall a sacrifice to the attempt. If the combination is not general, it will imply that some of the members are interested in that which is the cause of dissatisfaction to others, and this cannot be an attack upon the common liberty, but upon the interests of one part in favor of another part; and it will be a war between the members of the federal union with each other, not between them and the federal government. From the plainest principles of human nature, two inferences are to be drawn: one, that each member of a political confederacy will be more disposed to advance its own authority upon the ruins of that of the confederacy, than to make any improper concession in its favor, or support it in unreasonable pretensions; the other, that the subjects of each member will be more devoted in their attachments and obedience to their own particular governments, than to that of the union.

It is the temper of societies as well as of individuals to be impatient of constraint, and to prefer partial to general interest. Many cases may occur where members of a confederacy have, or seem to have, an advantage in things contrary to the good of the whole, or a disadvantage in others conducive to that end. The selfishness of every part will dispose each to believe that the public burdens are unequally apportioned, and that itself is the victim. These and other circumstances will promote a disposition for abridging the authority of the federal government; and the ambition of men in office in each state will make them glad to encourage it. They think their own consequence connected with the power of the government of which they are a part; and will endeavor to increase the one as the means of increasing the other.

The particular governments will have more empire over the minds of their subjects than the general one, because their agency will be more direct, more uniform, and more apparent. The people will be habituated to look up to them as the arbiters and guardians of their personal concerns, by which the passions of the vulgar, if not of all men, are most strongly affected; and in every difference with the confederated body, will side with them against the common sovereign.

Experience confirms the truth of these principles. The chief cities of Greece had once their council of Amphyctions, or States-general, with authority to decide and compose the differences of the several cities, and to transact many other important matters relative to the common interest and safety. At their first institution, they had great weight and credit; but never enough to preserve effectually the balance and harmony of the confederacy; and in time their decrees only served as an additional pretext to that side whose pretensions they favored. When the cities were not engaged in foreign wars, they were at perpetual variance among themselves. Sparta and Athens contended twenty-seven years for the precedence, or rather dominion, of Greece, till the former made herself mistress of the whole; and till, in subsequent struggles, having had recourse to the pernicious expedient of calling in the aid of foreign enemies, the Macedonians first and afterward the Romans became their masters.

The German Diet had formerly more authority than it now has, though like that of Greece never enough to hinder the great potentates from disturbing the repose of the empire, and mutually wasting their own territories and people.

The Helvetic League is another example. It is true it has subsisted nearly five hundred years; but in that period the cantons have had repeated and furious wars with each other, which would have made them an easy prey to their more powerful neighbors, had not the reciprocal jealousy of these prevented either from taking advantage of their dissensions. This and their poverty have hitherto saved them from total destruction, and kept them from feeling the miseries of foreign conquest, added to those of civil war. The federal government is too weak to hinder their renewal, whenever the ambition or fanaticism of the principal cantons shall be disposed to rekindle the flame. For some time past, indeed, it has been in a great measure nominal; the Protestants and Catholics have had separate diets, to manage almost all matters of importance; so that in fact, the general diet is only kept up to regulate the affairs of the common bailliages and preserve a semblance of union; and even this, it is probable would cease, did not the extreme weakness of the cantons oblige them to a kind of coalition.

If the divisions of the United Provinces have not proceeded to equal extremities, there are peculiar causes to be assigned. The authority of the Stadtholder pervades the whole frame of the republic, and is a kind of common link by which the provinces are bound together. The jealousy of his progressive influence, in which more or less they all agree, operates as a check upon their ill-humors against one another. The inconsiderableness of each province separately, and the imminent danger to which the whole would be exposed of being overrun by their neighbors in case of disunion, is a further preservative against the phrensy of hostility; and their importance and even existence depending entirely upon frugality, industry, and commerce, peace both at home and abroad is of necessity the predominant object of their policy.

NO. III

August 9, 1781.

The situation of these States is very unlike that of the United Provinces. Remote as we are from Europe, in a little time we should fancy ourselves out of the reach of attempts from abroad, and in full liberty, at our leisure and convenience, to try our strength at home. This might not happen at once, but if the Federal Government should lose its authority it would certainly follow. Political societies in close neighborhood must either be strongly united under one government, or there will infallibly exist emulations and quarrels; this is in human nature, and we have no reason to think ourselves wiser or better than other men. Some of the larger States, a small number of years hence, will be in themselves populous, rich, and powerful in all those circumstances calculated to inspire ambition and nourish ideas of separation and independence. Though it will ever be their true interest to preserve the Union, their vanity and self-importance will be very likely to overpower that motive, and make them seek to place themselves at the head of particular confederacies independent of the general one. A schism once introduced, competitions of boundary and rivalships of commerce will easily afford pretexts for war.

European powers may have many inducements for fomenting these divisions and playing us off against each other; but without such a disposition in them, if separations once take place we shall, of course, embrace different interests and connections. The particular confederacies, leaguing themselves with rival nations, will naturally be involved in their disputes, into which they will be the more readily tempted by the hope of making acquisitions upon each other and upon the colonies of the powers with whom they are respectively at enmity.

We already see symptoms of the evils to be apprehended. In the midst of a war for our existence as a nation—in the midst of dangers too serious to be trifled with, some of the States have evaded or refused compliance with the demands of Congress in points of the greatest moment to the common safety. If they act such a part at this perilous juncture, what are we to expect in a time of peace and security? Is it not to be feared that the resolutions of Congress would soon become like the decisions of the Greek Amphyctions, or like the edicts of a German Diet?

But as these evils are at a little distance, we may perhaps be insensible and short-sighted enough to disregard them. There are others that threaten our immediate safety. Our whole system is in disorder; our currency depreciated, till in many places it will hardly obtain a circulation at all; public credit at its lowest ebb; our army deficient in numbers, and unprovided with every thing; the Government, in its present condition, unable to command the means to pay, clothe, or feed their troops; the enemy making an alarming progress in the Southern States, lately in complete possession of two of them, though now in part rescued by the genius and exertions of a general without an army; a force under Cornwallis still formidable to Virginia.

We ought to blush to acknowledge that this is a true picture of our situation, when we reflect that the enemy's whole force in the United States, including their American levies and the late reinforcements, is little more than fourteen thousand effective men; that our population, by recent examination, has been found to be greater than at the commencement of the war; that the quantity of our specie has also increased; that the country abounds with all the necessaries of life, and has a sufficiency of foreign commodities, with a considerable and progressive commerce; that we have, beyond comparison, a better stock of warlike materials than when we began the contest, and an ally as willing as able to supply our further wants; and that we have on the spot five thousand auxiliary troops, paid and subsisted by that ally, to assist in our defence.

Nothing but a general disaffection of the people or mismanagement in their rulers can account for the figure we make, and for the distresses and perplexities we experience contending against so small a force.

Our enemies themselves must now be persuaded that the first is not the cause, and we know it is not. The most decided attachment of the people could alone have made them endure, without a convulsion, the successive shocks in our currency, added to the unavoidable inconveniences of war. There is perhaps not another nation in the world that would have shown equal patience and perseverance in similar circumstances. The enemy have now tried the temper of almost every part of America, and they can hardly produce in their ranks a thousand men who, without their arts and seductions, have voluntarily joined their standard. The miseries of a rigorous captivity may perhaps have added half as many more to the number of the American levies at this time in their armies. This small accession of force is the more extraordinary, as they have at some periods been apparently in the full tide of success, while every thing wore an aspect tending to infuse despondency into the people of this country. This has been remarkably the case in the Southern States.

They for a time had almost undisturbed possession of two of them, and Cornwallis, after overrunning a great part of a third, after two victorious battles, only brought with him into Virginia about two hundred Tories; in the State where he thought himself so well established, that he presumptuously ventured to assure the minister there was not a rebel left, a small body of continental troops have been so effectually seconded by the militia of that vanquished country as to have been able to capture a number of his troops more than equal to their own, and to repossess the principal part of the State.

As in the explanation of our embarrassments nothing can be alleged to the disaffection of the people, we must have recourse to the other cause—of impolicy and mismanagement in their rulers.

Where the blame of this may lie is not so much the question as what are the proper remedies, yet it may not be amiss to remark that too large a share has fallen upon Congress. That body is no doubt chargeable with mistakes, but perhaps its greatest has been too much readiness to make concessions of the powers implied in its original trust. This is partly to be attributed to an excessive complaisance to the spirit which has evidently actuated a majority of the States, a desire of monopolizing all power in themselves. Congress has been responsible for the administration of affairs, without the means of fulfilling that responsibility.

It would be too severe a reflection upon us to suppose that a disposition to make the most of the friendship of others, and to exempt ourselves from a full share of the burthens of the war, has had any part in the backwardness which has appeared in many of the States to confer powers and adopt measures adequate to the exigency. Such a sentiment would neither be wise, just, generous, nor honorable; nor do I believe the accusation would be well founded, yet our conduct makes us liable to a suspicion of this sort. It is certain, however, that too sanguine expectations from Europe have unintentionally relaxed our efforts by diverting a sense of danger, and begetting an opinion that the inequality of the contest would make every campaign the last.

We did not consider how difficult it must be to exhaust the resources of a nation circumstanced like that of Great Britain; whose government has always been distinguished for energy, and its people for enthusiasm. Nor did we in estimating the superiority of our friends make sufficient allowance for that want of concert which will ever characterize the operations of allies, or for the immense advantage to the enemy of having their forces, though inferior, under a single direction.

Finding the rest of Europe either friendly or pacific, we never calculated the contingencies which might alter that disposition; nor reflected that the death[1] of a single prince, the change or caprice of a single minister, was capable of giving a new face to the whole system.

We are at this time more sanguine than ever. The war with the Dutch,* we believe, will give such an addition of force to our side as will make the superiority irresistible. No person can dispute this, if things remain in their present state; but the extreme disparity of the contest is the very reason why this cannot be the case. The neutral powers will either effect a particular or a general accommodation, or they will take their sides. There are three suppositions to be made: one, that there will be a compromise *between the United Provinces* and England, for which we are certain the mediation of Austria and Russia has been offered; another, a pacification between all the belligerent powers, for which we have reason to believe the same mediation has been offered; the third, a rejection of the terms of mediation and a more general war.

Either of these suppositions is a motive for exertion. The first will place things in the same, probably in a worse, situation than before the declaration of the war against Holland. The composing of present differences may be accompanied with a revival of ancient connections; and

---

* Hamilton refers here to the outbreak of the Fourth Anglo-Dutch War (1780–84). See Jonathan Israel, *The Dutch Republic, 1477–1806* (Oxford, 1995), 1097.

1. The death of the Empress Queen has actually produced a change. Her politics, if not friendly to our connections, were at least pacific, and while she lived no hostile interference of the House of Austria was to be expected. The Emperor, her son, by her death left more at liberty to pursue his inclinations averse to the aggrandizement of France, of course afraid of the abasement of England, has given several indications of an unfriendly disposition. It should be a weighty consideration with us, that among the potentates which we look upon as amicable, three of the principal ones are at a very advanced stage of life—the King of Spain, the King of Prussia, and the Empress of Russia. We know not what may be the politics of successors.

at least would be productive of greater caution and restraint in a future intercourse with us.

The second, it is much to be dreaded, would hazard a dismemberment[2] of a part of these States; and we are bound in honor, in duty, and in interest, to employ every effort to dispossess the enemy of what they hold. A natural basis of the negotiation with respect to this continent will be, that each party shall retain what it possesses at the conclusion of the treaty, qualified perhaps by a cession of particular points for an equivalent elsewhere. It is too delicate to dwell on the motives to this apprehension; but if such a compromise sometimes terminates the disputes of nations originally independent, it will be less extraordinary where one party was originally under the dominion of the other.

2. Perhaps not expressly and directly, but virtually, under the plausible form of a new arrangement of limits.

If we are determined, as we ought to be with the concurrence of our allies, not to accept such a condition, then we ought to prepare for the third event—a more general and more obstinate war.

Should this take place a variety of new interests will be involved, and the affairs of America may cease to be of primary importance. In proportion as the objects and operations of the war become complicated and extensive, the final success must become uncertain; and in proportion as the interests of others in our concerns may be weakened or supplanted by more immediate interests of their own, ought our attention to ourselves and exertions in our own behalf to be awakened and augmented.

We ought, therefore, not only to strain every nerve for complying with the requisitions to render the present campaign as decisive as possible, but we ought without delay to enlarge the powers of Congress. Every plan of which this is not the foundation will be illusory. The separate exertions of the States will never suffice. Nothing but a well-proportioned exertion of the resources of the whole, under the direction of a common council, with power sufficient to give efficacy to their resolutions, can preserve us from being a conquered people now or can make us a happy people hereafter.

NO. IV

August 30, 1781.

The preceding numbers are chiefly intended to confirm an opinion, already pretty generally received, that it is necessary to augment the powers of the Confederation. The principal difficulty yet remains to fix the public judgment definitely on the points which ought to compose that augmentation.

It may be pronounced with confidence that nothing short of the following articles can suffice.

1st.—THE POWER OF REGULATING TRADE, comprehending a right of granting bounties and premiums by way of encouragement, of imposing duties of every kind as well for revenue as regulation, of appointing all officers of the customs, and of laying embargoes in extraordinary emergencies.

2d.—A moderate-levied tax, throughout the United States, of a specific rate per pound or per acre,[3] granted to the Federal Government in perpetuity, and, if Congress think proper, to be levied by their own collectors.

3d.—A moderate capitation-tax on every male[4] inhabitant above fifteen years of age, exclusive of common soldiers, common seamen, day laborers, cottagers, and paupers, to be also vested in perpetuity, and with the same condition of collection.

4th.—The disposal of all unlocated land for the benefit of the United States (so far as respects the profits of the first sale and the quit-rents), the jurisdiction remaining to the respective States in whose limits they are contained.

5th.—A certain proportion of the product of all mines discovered, or

---

3. Two pence an acre on cultivated, and a half-penny on uncultivated, land would answer the purpose, and would be so moderate as not to be felt; a small tax on uncultivated land would have the good effect of obliging the proprietor either to cultivate it himself or to dispose of it to some persons that would do it.

4. Suppose a dollar, or even half a dollar, per head.

to be discovered, for the same duration, and with the same right of collection as in the second and third articles.

6th.—The appointment of all land (as well as naval) officers of every rank.

The three first articles are of IMMEDIATE NECESSITY; the three last would be of great present, but of much greater future, utility; the whole combined would give solidity and permanency to the Union.

The great defect of the Confederation is, that it gives the United States no property; or, in other words, no revenue, nor the means of acquiring it, inherent in themselves and independent on the temporary pleasure of the different members. And power without revenue, in political society, is a name. While Congress continue altogether dependent on the occasional grants of the several States, for the means of defraying the expenses of the Federal Government, it can neither have dignity, vigor, nor credit. Credit supposes specific and permanent funds for the punctual payment of interest, with a moral certainty of the final redemption of the principal.

In our situation it will probably require more, on account of the general diffidence which has been excited by the past disorders in our finances. It will perhaps be necessary, in the first instance, to appropriate funds for the redemption of the principal in a determinate period, as well as for the payment of interest.

It is essential that the property in such funds should be in the contractor himself, and the appropriation dependent on his own will. If, instead of this, the possession or disposal of them is dependent on the voluntary or occasional concurrence of a number of different wills not under his absolute control, both the one and the other will be too precarious to be trusted. The most wealthy and best established nations are obliged to pledge their funds to obtain credit, and it would be the height of absurdity in us, in the midst of a revolution, to expect to have it on better terms. This credit being to be procured through Congress, the funds ought to be provided, declared, and vested in them.[5] It is a fact

5. It might, indeed, be a good restraint upon the spirit of running in debt, with which governments are too apt to be infected, to make it a condition of the grants to Congress,

that verifies the want of specific funds that the circumstance which operates powerfully against our obtaining credit abroad is, not a distrust of our becoming independent, but of our continuing united, and with our present Confederation the distrust is natural. Both foreigners and the thinking men among ourselves would have much more confidence in the duration of the Union, if they were to see it supported on the foundation here proposed.

There are some among us ignorant enough to imagine that the war may be carried on without credit, defraying the expenses of the year with what may be raised within the year. But this is for want of a knowledge of our real resources and expenses.

It may be demonstrated that the whole amount of the revenue which these States are capable of affording will be deficient annually five or six millions of dollars for the support of civil government and of the war.

This is not a conjecture hazarded at random, but the result of experiment and calculation; nor can it appear surprising, when it is considered that the revenues of the United Provinces, equal to these States in population, beyond comparison superior in industry, commerce, and riches, do not exceed twenty-five millions of guilders, or about nine millions and a half of dollars. In times of war they have raised a more considerable sum, but it has been chiefly by gratuitous combinations of rich individuals, a resource we cannot employ, because there are few men of large fortunes in this country, and these for the most part are in land. Taxes in the United Provinces are carried to an extreme which would be impracticable here. Not only the living are made to pay for every necessary of life, but even the dead are tributary to the public for the liberty of interment at particular hours. These considerations make it evident that we could not raise an equal amount of revenue in these States. Yet, in '76, when the currency was not depreciated, Congress emitted, for the expenses of the year, fourteen millions of dollars. It cannot be denied

---

that they shall be obliged, in all their loans, to appropriate funds for the payment of principal as well as interest, and such a restriction might be serviceable to public credit.

that there was a want of order and economy in the expenditure of public money, nor that we had a greater military force to maintain at that time than we now have; but, on the other hand, allowing for the necessary increase in our different civil lists, and for the advanced prices of many articles, it can hardly be supposed possible to reduce our annual expense very much below that sum. This simple idea of the subject, without entering into details, may satisfy us that the deficiency which has been stated is not to be suspected of exaggeration.

Indeed, nations the most powerful and opulent are obliged to have recourse to loans in time of war, and hence it is that most of the states of Europe are deeply immersed in debt. France is among the number, notwithstanding her immense population, wealth, and resources. England owes the enormous sum of two hundred millions sterling. The United Provinces, with all their prudence and parsimony, owe a debt of the generality of fifty millions, besides the particular debts of each province. Almost all the other powers are more or less in the same circumstances.

While this teaches us how contracted and uninformed are the views of those who expect to carry on the war without running in debt, it ought to console us with respect to the amount of that which we now owe, or may have occasion to incur in the remainder of the war. The whole, without burthening the people, may be paid off in twenty years after the conclusion of peace.

The principal part of the deficient five or six millions must be procured by loans from private persons at home and abroad. Every thing may be hoped from the generosity of France which her means will permit, but she has full employment for her revenues and credit in the prosecution of the war on her own part. If we judge of the future by the past, the pecuniary succors from her must continue to be far short of our wants, and the contingency of a war on the continent of Europe makes it possible they may diminish rather than increase.

We have in a less degree experienced the friendship of Spain in this article.

The Government of the United Provinces, if disposed to do it, can give us no assistance. The resources of the republic are chiefly mortgaged for former debts. Happily, it has extensive credit, but it will have occasion for the whole to supply its own exigencies.

Private men, either foreigners or natives, will not lend to a large amount, but on the usual security of funds properly established. This security Congress cannot give till the several States vest them with revenue, or the means of revenue, for that purpose.

Congress have[6] wisely appointed a superintendent of their finances, a man of acknowledged abilities and integrity, as well as of great personal credit and pecuniary influence.

It was impossible that the business of finance could be ably conducted by a body of men however well composed or well intentioned. Order in the future management of our moneyed concerns, a strict regard to the performance of public engagements, and of course the restoration of public credit may be reasonably and confidently expected from Mr. Morris' administration if he is furnished with materials upon which to operate—that is, if the Federal Government can acquire funds as the basis of his arrangements. He has very judiciously proposed a National Bank, which, by uniting the influence and interest of the moneyed men with the resources of government, can alone give it that durable and extensive credit of which it stands in need. This is the best expedient he could have devised for relieving the public embarrassments, but to give success to the plan it is essential that Congress should have it in their power to support him with unexceptionable funds. Had we begun the practice of funding four years ago, we should have avoided that depreciation of the currency which has been pernicious to the morals and to the credit of the nation, and there is no other method than this to prevent a continuance and multiplication of the evils flowing from that prolific source.

6. Robert Morris.

NO. V

April 18, 1782.

The vesting Congress with the power of regulating trade ought to have been a principal object of the Confederation for a variety of reasons. It is as necessary for the purposes of commerce as of revenue. There are some who maintain that trade will regulate itself, and is not to be benefited by the encouragements or restraints of government. Such persons will imagine that there is no need of a common directing power. This is one of those wild speculative paradoxes, which have grown into credit among us, contrary to the uniform practice and sense of the most enlightened nations.

Contradicted by the numerous institutions and laws that exist everywhere for the benefit of trade, by the pains taken to cultivate particular branches and to discourage others, by the known advantages derived from those measures, and by the palpable evils that would attend their discontinuance, it must be rejected by every man acquainted with commercial history. Commerce, like other things, has its fixed principles, according to which it must be regulated. If these are understood and observed, it will be promoted by the attention of government; if unknown, or violated, it will be injured—but it is the same with every other part of administration.

To preserve the balance of trade in favor of a nation ought to be a leading aim of its policy. The avarice of individuals may frequently find its account in pursuing channels of traffic prejudicial to that balance, to which the government may be able to oppose effectual impediments. There may, on the other hand, be a possibility of opening new sources, which, though accompanied with great difficulties in the commencement, would in the event amply reward the trouble and expense of bringing them to perfection. The undertaking may often exceed the influence and capitals of individuals, and may require no small assistance, as well from the revenue as from the authority of the state.

The contrary opinion, which has grown into a degree of vogue among us, has originated in the injudicious attempts made at different times to effect a regulation of prices. It became a cant phrase among the opposers of these attempts, that trade must regulate itself; by which at first was only meant that it had its fundamental laws, agreeable to which its general operations must be directed, and that any violent attempts in opposition to these would commonly miscarry. In this sense the maxim was reasonable, but it has since been extended to militate against all interference by the sovereign; an extreme as little reconcilable with experience or common sense as the practice it was first framed to discredit.

The reasonings of a very ingenious and sensible writer,[7] by being misapprehended, have contributed to this mistake. The scope of his argument is not, as by some supposed, that trade will hold a certain invariable course independent on the aid, protection, care, or concern of government; but that it will, in the main, depend upon the comparative industry, moral and physical advantages of nations; and that though, for a while, from extraordinary causes, there may be a wrong balance against one of them, this will work its own cure, and things will ultimately return to their proper level.* His object was to combat that excessive jealousy on this head, which has been productive of so many unnecessary wars, and with which the British nation is particularly infected; but it was no part of his design to insinuate that the regulating hand of government was either useless or hurtful. The nature of a government, its spirit, maxims, and laws, with respect to trade, are among those constant moral causes which influence its general results, and when it has by accident taken a wrong direction, assist in bringing it back to its natural course. This is everywhere admitted by all writers upon the subject; nor is there one who has asserted a contrary doctrine.

---

* The reference, very much confused, is to Hume's famous statement of the specie flow mechanism in "Of the Balance of Trade," *Essays,* 311–12, which he conflates with Hume's statement of the mutual gains from trade in "Of the Jealousy of Trade," *ibid.,* 327–31.

7. Hume's essay: *Jealousy of Trade.*

Trade may be said to have taken its rise in England under the auspices of Elizabeth, and its rapid progress there is in a great measure to be ascribed to the fostering care of government in that and succeeding reigns.

From a different spirit in the government, with superior advantages, France was much later in commercial improvements; nor would her trade have been at this time in so prosperous a condition, had it not been for the abilities and indefatigable endeavors of the great Colbert. He laid the foundation of the French commerce, and taught the way to his successors to enlarge and improve it. The establishment of the woollen manufacture in a kingdom where nature seemed to have denied the means, is one, among many proofs, how much may be effected in favor of commerce by the attention and patronage of a wise administration.

The number of useful edicts passed by Louis XIV., and since his time, in spite of frequent interruptions from the jealous enmity of Great Britain, has advanced that of France to a degree which has excited the envy and astonishment of its neighbors.

The Dutch, who may justly be allowed a pre-eminence in the knowledge of trade, have ever made it an essential object of state. Their commercial regulations are more rigid and numerous than those of any other country; and it is by a judicious and unremitted vigilance of government that they have been able to extend their traffic to a degree so much beyond their natural and comparative advantages.

Perhaps it may be thought that the power of regulation will be best placed in the governments of the several States, and that a general superintendence is unnecessary. If the States had distinct interests, were unconnected with each other, their own governments would then be the proper, and could be the only, depositories of such a power; but as they are parts of a whole, with a common interest in trade, as in other things, there ought to be a common direction in that as in all other matters. It is easy to conceive that many cases may occur in which it would be beneficial to all the States to encourage or suppress a particular branch of trade, while it would be detrimental to either to attempt it without the concurrence of the rest, and where the experiment would probably be left untried for fear of a want of that concurrence.

No mode can be so convenient as a source of revenue to the United States. It is agreed that imposts on trade, when not immoderate, or improperly laid, are one of the most eligible species of taxation. They fall in a great measure upon articles not of absolute necessity, and being partly transferred to the price of the commodity, are so far imperceptibly paid by the consumer. It is therefore that mode which may be exercised by the Federal Government with least exception or disgust. Congress can easily possess all the information necessary to impose the duties with judgment, and the collection can without difficulty be made by their own officers.

They can have no temptation to abuse this power, because the motive of revenue will check its own extremes. Experience has shown that moderate duties are more productive than high ones. When they are low, a nation can trade abroad on better terms, its imports and exports will be larger, the duties will be regularly paid, and arising on a greater quantity of commodities, will yield more in the aggregate than when they are so high as to operate either as a prohibition, or as an inducement to evade them by illicit practices.

It is difficult to assign any good reason why Congress should be more liable to abuse the powers with which they are entrusted than the State Assemblies. The frequency of the election of the members is a full security against a dangerous ambition, and the rotation established by the Confederation makes it impossible for any state, by continuing the same men, who may put themselves at the head of a prevailing faction, to maintain for any length of time an undue influence in the national councils. It is to be presumed that Congress will be in general better composed for abilities, as well as for integrity, than any assembly on the continent.

But to take away any temptation from a cabal to load particular articles, which are the principal objects of commerce to particular States, with a too great proportion of duties, to ease the others in the general distribution of expense, let all the duties, whether for regulation or revenue, raised in each State, be credited to that State, and let it, in like manner, be charged for all the bounties paid within itself for the encouragement of agriculture, manufactures, or trade. This expedient will remove the temptation; for as the quotas of the respective States are to be determined by a standard of land, agreeable to the eighth article of the Confederation, each will have so much the less to contribute otherwise, as it pays more on its commerce. An objection has been made in a late instance to this principle. It has been urged that as the consumer pays the duty, those States which are not equally well situated for foreign commerce, and which consume a great part of the imports of their neighbors, will become contributors to a part of their taxes. This objection is rather specious than solid.

The maxim, that the consumer pays the duty, has been admitted in theory with too little reserve; frequently contradicted in practice. It is true, the merchant will be unwilling to let the duty be a deduction from his profits, if the state of the market will permit him to incorporate it with the price of his commodity. But this is often not practicable. It turns upon the quantity of goods at market in proportion to the demand. When the latter exceeds the former, and the competition is among the buyers, the merchant can easily increase his price, and make his customers pay the duty. When the reverse is the case, and the competition is among the sellers, he must then content himself with smaller profits and lose the value of the duty, or at least a part of it. When a nation has a flourishing and well-settled trade, this more commonly happens than may be imagined, and it will, many times, be found that the duty is divided between the merchant and the consumer.

Besides this consideration which greatly diminishes the force of the objection, there is another which entirely destroys it. There is a strong reciprocal influence between the prices of all commodities in a State, by which they, sooner or later, attain a pretty exact balance and proportion to each other. If the immediate productions of the soil rise, the manufacturer will have more for his manufacture, the merchant for his goods; and the same will happen with whatever class the increase of price begins.

If duties are laid upon the imports in one State, by which the prices of foreign articles are raised, the products of land and labor within that State will take a proportionate rise; and if a part of those articles are consumed in a neighboring State, it will have the same influence there as at home. The importing State must allow an advanced price upon the commodities which it receives in exchange from its neighbor, in a ratio to the increased price of the article it sells. To know, then, which is the gainer or loser, we must examine how the general balance of trade stands between them. If the importing State takes more of the commodities of its neighbor than it gives in exchange, that will be the loser by the reciprocal augmentation of prices; it will be the gainer if it takes less, and neither will gain or lose if the barter is carried on upon equal terms. The balance of trade, and consequently the gain, or loss, in this respect, will be governed more by the relative industry and frugality of the parties than by their relative advantages for foreign commerce.

Between separate nations this reasoning will not apply with full force, because a multitude of local and extraneous circumstances may counteract the principle; but from the intimate connections of these States, the similitude of governments, situations, customs, manners, political and commercial causes will have nearly the same operation in the intercourse between the States, as in that between the different parts of the same State. If this should be controverted, the objection drawn from the hypothesis of the consumer paying the duty must fall at the same time; for as far as this is true it is as much confined in its application to a State within itself as the doctrine of a reciprocal proportion of prices.

General principles in subjects of this nature ought always to be advanced with caution; in an experimental analysis there are found such a number of exceptions as tend to render them very doubtful; and in questions which affect the existence and collective happiness of these States, all nice and abstract distinctions should give way to plainer interests, and to more obvious and simple rules of conduct.

But the objection which has been urged ought to have no weight on another account. Which are the States that have not sufficient advantages for foreign commerce, and that will not in time be their own carriers? Connecticut and Jersey are the least maritime of the whole; yet the Sound which washes the coast of Connecticut has an easy outlet to the ocean, affords a number of harbors and bays very commodious for trading vessels. New London may be a receptacle for merchantmen of almost any burthen; and the fine rivers with which the State is intersected, by facilitating the transportation of commodities to and from every part, are extremely favorable both to its domestic and foreign trade.

Jersey, by way of Amboy, has a shorter communication with the ocean than the city of New York. Prince's Bay, which may serve as an outport to it, will admit and shelter in winter and summer vessels of any size. Egg Harbor, on its southern coast, is not to be despised. The Delaware may be made as subservient to its commerce as to that of Pennsylvania, Gloucester, Burlington, and Trenton, being all conveniently situated on that river. The United Provinces, with inferior advantages of position to either of these States, have for centuries held the first rank among commercial nations.

The want of large trading cities has been sometimes objected as an obstacle to the commerce of these States; but this is a temporary deficiency that will repair itself with the increase of population and riches. The reason that the States in question have hitherto carried on little foreign trade, is that they have found it equally beneficial to purchase the commodities imported by their neighbors. If the imposts on trade should work an inconvenience to them, it will soon cease by making it their interest to trade abroad.

It is too much characteristic of our national temper to be ingenious in finding out and magnifying the minutest disadvantages, and to reject measures of evident utility, even of necessity, to avoid trivial and sometimes imaginary evils. We seem not to reflect that in human society there is scarcely any plan, however salutary to the whole and to every part, by the share each has in the common prosperity, but in one way, or another, and under particular circumstances, will operate more to the benefit of some parts than of others. Unless we can overcome this narrow disposition and learn to estimate measures by their general tendencies, we shall never be a great or a happy people, if we remain a people at all.

NO. VI

July 4, 1782.

Let us see what will be the consequences of not authorizing the Federal Government to regulate the trade of these States. Besides the want of revenue and of power, besides the immediate risk to our independence and the dangers of all the future evils of a precarious Union, besides the deficiency of a wholesome concert and provident superintendence to advance the general prosperity of trade, the direct consequence will be that the landed interest and the laboring poor will in the first place fall a sacrifice to the trading interest, and the whole eventually to a bad system of policy made necessary by the want of such regulating power.

Each State will be afraid to impose duties on its commerce, lest the other States, not doing the same, should enjoy greater advantages than itself, by being able to afford native commodities cheaper abroad and foreign commodities cheaper at home.

A part of the evils resulting from this would be a loss to the revenue of those moderate duties which, without being injurious to commerce, are allowed to be the most agreeable species of taxes to the people. Articles of foreign luxury, while they would contribute nothing to the income of the State, being less dear by an exemption from duties, would have a more extensive consumption.

Many branches of trade, hurtful to the common interest, would be continued for want of proper checks and discouragements. As revenues must be found to satisfy the public exigencies in peace and in war, too great a proportion of taxes will fall directly upon land, and upon the necessaries of life—the produce of that land. The influence of these evils will be to render landed property fluctuating and less valuable; to oppress the poor by raising the prices of necessaries; to injure commerce by encouraging the consumption of foreign luxuries, by increasing the value of labor, by lessening the quantity of home productions, enhancing their prices at foreign markets, of course obstructing their sale, and enabling other nations to supplant us.

Particular caution ought at present to be observed in this country not to burthen the soil itself and its productions with heavy impositions, because the quantity of unimproved land will invite the husbandman to abandon old settlements for new, and the disproportion of our population for some time to come will necessarily make labor dear, to reduce which, and not to increase it, ought to be a capital object of our policy.

Easy duties, therefore, on commerce, especially on imports, ought to lighten the burthens which will unavoidably fall upon land. Though it may be said that, on the principle of a reciprocal influence of prices, whereon the taxes are laid in the first instance, they will in the end be borne by all classes, yet it is of the greatest importance that no one should sink under the immediate pressure. The great art is to distribute the public burthens well, and not suffer them, either first or last, to fall too heavily on parts of the community, else distress and disorder must ensue; a shock given to any part of the political machine vibrates through the whole.

As a sufficient revenue could not be raised from trade to answer the public purposes, other articles have been proposed. A moderate land and poll tax, being of easy and unexpensive collection, and leaving nothing to discretion, are the simplest and best that could be devised.

It is to be feared that the avarice of many of the landholders will be opposed to a perpetual tax upon land, however moderate. They will ignorantly hope to shift the burthens of the national expense from themselves to others—a disposition as iniquitous as it is fruitless. The public necessities must be satisfied; this can only be done by the contributions of the whole society. Particular classes are neither able nor will they be willing to pay for the protection and security of the others, and where so selfish a spirit discovers itself in any member, the rest of the community will unite to compel it to do its duty.

Indeed, many theorists in political economy have held that all taxes, wherever they originate, fall upon land, and have therefore been of opinion that it would be best to draw the whole revenue of the state immediately from that source, to avoid the expense of a more diversified collection, and the accumulations which will be heaped, in their several stages, upon the primitive sums, advanced in those stages, which are imposed on our trade. But though it has been demonstrated that this theory has been carried to an extreme impracticable in fact, yet it is evident, in tracing the matter, that a large part of all taxes, however remotely laid, will, by an insensible circulation, come at last to settle upon land—the source of most of the materials employed in commerce.

It appears, from calculation made by the ablest master of political arithmetic, about sixty years ago, that the yearly product of all the lands in England amounted to £42,000,000 sterling, and the whole annual consumption at that period, of foreign as well as domestic commodities, did not exceed £49,000,000, and the surplus of the exportation above the importation £2,000,000, on which sums arise all the revenues, in whatever shape, which go into the Treasury. It is easy to infer from this how large a part of them must, directly or indirectly, be derived from land.

Nothing can be more mistaken than the collision and rivalship which almost always subsist between the landed and trading interests, for the truth is they are so inseparably interwoven that one cannot be injured without injury nor benefited without benefit to the other. Oppress trade, lands sink in value; make it flourish, their value rises. Incumber husbandry, trade declines; encourage agriculture, commerce revives. The progress of this mutual reaction might be easily delineated, but it is too obvious to every man who turns his thoughts, however superficially, upon the subject to require it. It is only to be regretted that it is too often lost sight of when the seductions of some immediate advantage or exemption tempt us to sacrifice the future to the present.

But perhaps the class is more numerous of those who, not unwilling to bear their share of public burthens, are yet averse to the idea of perpetuity, as if there ever would arrive a period when the state would cease to want revenues and taxes become unnecessary. It is of importance to unmask this delusion, and open the eyes of the people to the truth. It is paying too great a tribute to the idol of popularity, to flatter so injurious and so visionary an expectation. The error is too gross to be tolerated anywhere but in the cottage of the peasant. Should we meet with it in the Senate-house, we must lament the ignorance or despise the hypocrisy on which it is ingrafted. Expense is in the present state of things entailed upon all governments; though, if we continue united, we shall be hereafter less exposed to wars by land than most other countries; yet while we have powerful neighbors on either extremity, and our frontier is embraced by savages whose alliance they may without difficulty command, we cannot, in prudence, dispense with the usual precautions for our interior security. As a commercial people, maritime power must be a primary object of our attention, and a navy cannot be created or maintained without ample revenues. The nature of our popular institutions requires a numerous magistracy, for whom competent provision must be made, or we may be certain our affairs will always be committed to improper hands, and experience will teach us that no government costs so much as a bad one.

We may preach, till we are tired of the theme, the necessity of disinterestedness in republics, without making a single proselyte. The virtuous declaimer will neither persuade himself nor any other person to be content with a double mess of pottage, instead of a reasonable stipend for his services. We might as soon reconcile ourselves to the Spartan community of goods and wives, to their iron coin, their long beards, or their black broth. There is a total dissimilarity in the circumstances as well as the manners of society among us, and it is as ridiculous to seek for models in the small ages of Greece and Rome, as it would be to go in quest of them among the Hottentots and Laplanders.

The public, for the different purposes that have been mentioned, must always have large demands upon its constituents, and the only question is, whether these shall be satisfied by annual grants perpetually renewed, by a perpetual grant once for all, or by a compound of permanent and occasional supplies. The last is the wisest course. The Federal Government should neither be independent nor too much dependent. It should neither be raised above responsibility or control, nor should it want the means of maintaining its own weight, authority, dignity, and credit. To this end, permanent funds are indispensable, but they ought to be of such a nature and so moderate in their amount as never to be inconvenient. Extraordinary supplies can be the objects of extraordinary emergencies, and in that salutary medium will consist our true wisdom.

It would seem as if no mode of taxation could be relished but the worst of all modes, which now prevails—by assessment. Every proposal for a specific tax is sure to meet with opposition. It has been objected to a poll tax at a fixed rate, that it will be unequal, and the rich will pay no more than the poor. In the form in which it has been offered in these papers, the poor, properly speaking, are not comprehended, though it is true that beyond the exclusion of the indigent the tax has no reference to the proportion of property, but it should be remembered that it is impossible to devise any specific tax that will operate equally on the whole community. It must be the province of the Legislature to hold the scales with a judicious hand and balance one by another. The rich must be made to pay for their luxuries, which is the only proper way of taxing their superior wealth.

Do we imagine that our assessments operate equally? Nothing can be more contrary to the fact. Wherever a discretionary power is lodged in any set of men over the property of their neighbors, they will abuse it; their passions, prejudices, partialities, dislikes, will have the principal lead in measuring the abilities of those over whom their power extends; and assessors will ever be a set of petty tyrants, too unskilful, if honest, to be possessed of so delicate a trust, and too seldom honest to give them the excuse of want of skill.

The genius of liberty reprobates every thing arbitrary or discretionary in taxation. It exacts that every man, by a definite and general rule, should know what proportion of his property the state demands; whatever liberty we may boast in theory, it cannot exist in fact while assessments continue.

The admission of them among us is a new proof how often human conduct reconciles the most glaring opposites; in the present case, the most vicious practice of despotic governments with the freest constitutions and the greatest love of liberty.

The establishment of permanent funds would not only answer the public purposes infinitely better than temporary supplies, but it would be the most effectual way of easing the people.

With this basis for procuring credit, the amount of present taxes might be greatly diminished. Large sums of money might be borrowed abroad at a low interest, and introduced into the country, to defray the current expenses and pay the public debts; which would not only lessen the demand for immediate supplies, but would throw more money into circulation, and furnish the people with greater means of paying the taxes.

Though it be a just rule that we ought not to run in debt to avoid present expense, so far as our faculties extend, yet the propriety of doing it cannot be disputed when it is apparent that these are incompetent to the public necessities. Efforts beyond our abilities can only tend to individual distress and national disappointment. The product of the three foregoing articles will be as little as can be required to enable Congress to pay their debts and restore order into their finances. In addition to them:

The disposal of the unlocated lands will hereafter be a valuable source of revenue and an immediate one of credit. As it may be liable to the same condition with the duties on trade—that is, the product of the sales within each State to be credited to that State—and as the rights of jurisdiction are not infringed, it seems to be susceptible of no reasonable objection.

Mines in every country constitute a branch of revenue. In this, where nature has so richly impregnated the bowels of the earth, they may in time become a valuable one; and as they require the care and attention of government to bring them to perfection, this care and a share in the profits of it will very properly devolve upon Congress. All the precious metals should absolutely be the property of the Federal Government, and with respect to the others it should have a discretionary power of reserving, in the nature of a tax, such part as it may judge not inconsistent with the encouragement due to so important an object. This is rather a future than a present resource.

The reason of allowing Congress to appoint its own officers of the customs, collectors of the taxes, and military officers of every rank, is to create in the interior of each State a mass of influence in favor of the Federal Government. The great danger has been shown to be that it will not have power enough to defend itself and preserve the Union, not that it will ever become formidable to the general liberty; a mere regard to the interests of the Confederacy will never be a principle sufficiently active to crush the ambition and intrigues of different members. Force cannot effect it. A contest of arms will seldom be between the common sovereign and a single refractory member, but between distinct combinations of the several parts against each other. A sympathy of situations will be apt to produce associates to the disobedient. The application of force is always disagreeable—the issue uncertain. It will be wise to obviate the necessity of it, by interesting such a number of individuals in each State in support of the Federal Government as will be counterpoised to the ambition of others, and will make it difficult for them to unite the people in opposition to the first and necessary measures of the Union.

There is something noble and magnificent in the perspective of a great Federal Republic, closely linked in the pursuit of a common interest, tranquil and prosperous at home, respectable abroad; but there is something proportionably diminutive and contemptible in the prospect of a number of petty States, with the appearance only of union, jarring, jealous, and perverse, without any determined direction, fluctuating and unhappy at home, weak and insignificant by their dissensions in the eyes of other nations.

Happy America, if those to whom thou hast intrusted the guardianship of thy infancy know how to provide for thy future repose, but miserable and undone, if their negligence or ignorance permits the spirit of discord to erect her banner on the ruins of thy tranquillity!

INDEX

This book is set in Adobe Caslon. Drawn in 1990 by Carol Twombly, it is based on faces cut in the 1720s and '30s by the English typefounder and designer William Caslon. A sturdy face possessed of great charm and simplicity, Caslon was the first typeface to be used in the American colonies. Revolutionary War broadsides, including the Declaration of Independence, and the first books printed in America were set in Caslon.

This book is printed on paper that is acid-free and meets the requirements of the American National Standard for Permanence of Paper for Printed Library Materials, z39.48-1992. ∞

Book Design by Erin Kirk New, Watkinsville, Georgia
Typography by Apex CoVantage, Madison, Wisconsin
Printed and bound by Worzalla Publishing Company,
Stevens Point, Wisconsin